What Others Are Saying About *Mud & Poetry*

If only Saint Augustine had grown up blogging, he too could have written this book. Either way, though, I'm pretty sure the good Augustine would resonate with Tyler Blanski's twenty-first-century confessions.
—Phyllis Tickle
Author and Lecturer

Tyler Blanski is a fresh voice in faith and spirituality. He is a friend and well worth listening to.

—Doug Pagitt
Author of *Church in the Inventive Age*

Mud and Poetry is a bold first work packed with earthy honesty and passionate longing. Tyler Blanski proves he's not only a singer; he can also write. And what he says in these pages—by turns zesty, grave, funny, airy, and frank—is well worth listening to and learning from. Here are the notes of Christian hope.

—Michael Ward
Author of *Planet Narnia: The Seven Heavens in the Imagination of C. S. Lewis*
Chaplain, St. Peter's College, Oxford

Mud and Poetry is a humble meditation on things that matter by a young man who writes honestly about his ventures into life and faith, and his is a voice we should listen to.

—Tony Jones
Author of *The New Christians: Dispatches from the Emergent Frontier*

Blanski's book, told in gritty, lyrical language, welcomes you to delve into the messy and wonderful expressions of Christian sex and marriage. He shows that a Christian single's walk of faith can be a purposeful journey into a deeper communion with Christ. Blanski understands that the through-thick-and-thin promise is fulfilled in moments of joys, trials, everydayness, and grace. As one happily married for thirty-plus years, I can say he got it right. He beautifully illustrates the duality of humanness, that we are both mud and poetry: needy biology and a spiritual, creative reflection of our Creator.

—Megan DiMaria
Author of *Searching for Spice* and *Out of Her Hands*

Can a young single Christian guy write a great book about sex and marriage? Tyler Blanski has done it! This book is fun but practical, very well-written, with a wonderful lyrical rhythm. Even an old fart like me, married for thirty-two years, found it helpful.

—Nate Larkin
Founder of the Samson Society and author of *Samson and the Pirate Monks: Calling Men to Authentic Brotherhood*

MUD & POETRY

love, sex, and the sacred

tyler blanski

FRESH AIR BOOKS®

Fresh Air Books Web site: www.freshairbooks.org

FRESH AIR BOOKS and design logos are trademarks owned by The Upper Room®, a ministry of GBOD®, Nashville, Tennessee. All rights reserved.

Unless otherwise indicated, scripture quotations are from the New Revised Standard Version Bible, copyright © 1989 National Council of the Churches of Christ in the United States of America. Used by permission. All rights reserved.
An extension of the copyright page appears on page 192-93.

In this book, some real-life conversations have been transposed into one, and a few of my dear friends have been condensed into a single character. All names are made up. Fortunately, no one has been compressed in real life: only in my book, and only for the sake of continuity, clarity, and especially for the sake of privacy.

Cover images: Sky and background: © Patrick Voigt/Corbis; Minneapolis skyline: Steve Lyon/flickr.com
Cover design: Left Coast Design, Portland, OR / www.lcoast.com
Interior design: PerfecType, Nashville, TN
First printing: 2010

Library of Congress Cataloging-in-Publication Data
Blanski, Tyler.
 Mud & poetry : love, sex, and the sacred / Tyler Blanski.
   p. cm.
Includes bibliographical references.
ISBN 978-1-935205-09-8
1. Christianity—Miscellanea. I. Title. II. Title: Mud and poetry.
BR124.B53 2010
230—dc22   2010019938

Printed in the United States of America

Some of the behaviors and opinions mentioned in this book might be troublesome to some readers. The publisher does not endorse or condone behaviors that can be injurious to one's physical or emotional wellbeing, and trusts that readers will seek professional counsel when necessary.

CONTENTS

FOREWORD

Regarding the use of earthly images, Christian spirituality has been of two minds: negation and affirmation. The first, because of God's transcendence, stressed the grand dissimilarity between the Creator and all he ever made. It dismissed earthly images as inadequate, even downright misleading. God, said its best practitioners, is a thought beyond all thinking, a word beyond all utterance, a vision beyond all seeing, and a being beyond all existence. Finite things cannot and do not reveal God; they hide him, the negationists insisted. God is ineffably different from the world. Between it and him there exists no reliable analogy.

Not so, said the pilgrims of the other path. Just as something of the painter is revealed in the paintings, and just as something of the poet is revealed in the poems, so something of the Creator is revealed in the creation. Let those who have ears to hear, hear; let those who have eyes to see, see.

While both the paths have led, by quite different routes, to godliness and to God, my concern, like the concern of this book, is with the second, the way of affirmation. That path is wondrously indirect and differentiated. Some saints, like Bonaventure, and some poets, like Wordsworth, affirm and explicate the images of nature at large.

7

They explain how nature and the multiform objects that it comprises are books, or ladders, or images that come from God and lead to God. These natural objects are, as it were, God's own commentaries, or guidebooks, to himself.

Other Christian thinkers, like Dante and Petrarch, affirm a different set of images, namely the images of romance. So also does this book by Tyler Blanski. It charts for us today the path charted earlier by them. The details and genre are different; the point is not. He tells in contemporary prose the poetic tale told centuries ago by others.

Nature has been deeply interfused with a homing instinct. Natural things incline toward where they belong, their natural habitat. Because it is drawn by unseen magnetic forces, the needle of a compass, if unimpeded, always points toward magnetic north. Pigeons, some say by means of that same magnetic force, find their way home, often across enormous distances. I myself once knew a dog that, weeks after it was lost, somehow found its way home from the other side of a neighboring state, across the Mississippi River.

Even so the human heart, when unimpeded, tends toward God. It too has a natural homing instinct. The German mystics called it *seelengrund*, the Greeks *synteresis*, the Latins *scintilla*, and the English "the spark of the soul." Whatever its name, because of sin it fails to work as it ought. It needs the grace of God. That grace comes in many forms and with many faces. The face God gives it is the face most congenial to your soul, the face most likely to open your eyes and awaken your sleeping heart. For many men, it is the face of a woman. For many women, it is the face of a man. That man, or that woman, because he or she is a human being and is beloved, is to us an image of the God from whom, by our evil, we have fled, but to whom, if we desire, we can return. As Dante showed us in *The Divine Comedy*, the difference between heaven and hell can be how well we follow our God-given images, how well we love our loves.

To see those images aright, we need to see three things accurately: the beloved as she is, the beloved as she shall be, and the Grand Love of whom she is the image. No delusions will do. The God who is Truth himself cannot be approached but by grace-induced clarity of mind and of vision. Put another way, because she is God's picture to our souls, we need to study the image as carefully as we would, say, Thomas's *Summa* or Calvin's *Institutes*. But where those things are the abstract, the beloved is the living, though fallen, embodiment. She is the human portrait; they are diagrams. She is to our hearts, to use an ancient Christian phrase, the God-bearer. We learn to love her as she is, and we learn to love what she shall become, so that we can learn to love the God whom she reflects—and learn to love like the God whom she reflects. In that way, romance is the practice field upon which we learn to cherish our Maker by learning to love the living image and reminder of himself that he has set before us.

As Helmut Thielicke once observed, this world is a house, lit by God, to help us find him. For some, God has set that light in the beloved, in the image, and like a beacon on a rocky and windswept coast, she can, if we see in her the bright image that she is, lead us safely to harbor: Dante again.

I have said that we must see her as she is, and that she is flawed. Though her flaws are real and not insignificant (no sin ever is), for her to function as the heart's image of God, those flaws are easily, almost naturally, overlooked. The world, after all, is full of love songs, all praising the perfections of imperfect persons, proving this is so. Lovers, like the mothers of delinquent children, seem naturally to find the lovely and the lovable in even the most unlovely creatures. In that sense, romance is like agape. It teaches us to practice, at least as regards one person, what agape desires for us to practice toward them all. It also teaches that while she might be more spirited than spiritual, might be careless and not just carefree, that she is the very image of the Eternal Love that made us and redeemed us. Romance helps us to see beyond what is to what shall be, to see the possible and the eventual in the actual, and to see that the dear perfections she now has will one day be all the more wonderful and all the more beautiful—because she will be all the more like God. Even more than she is now, she someday shall be more fully the image of the One Thing your soul delights in and longs for, though perhaps it does not know yet who that is or why.

God has wrapped his beauty, his love, his joy, and his compelling attractiveness in both the natural and the supernatural graces of the beloved. Because he has, the needle of our heart's compass, drawn as it is to the image, imperfect though she might be, begins to point a little more toward magnetic north than once it did. Through her, the Pied Piper of heaven pipes his magic song, and we are drawn closer to our eternal home.

For more of that story, read on.

—Michael Bauman
Professor of Theology and Culture, Hillsdale College
Scholar in Residence, Summit Semester

I, too, saw God through mud—
The mud that cracked on cheeks
when wretches smiled.

—WILFRED OWEN, "APOLOGIA PRO POEMATE MEO"

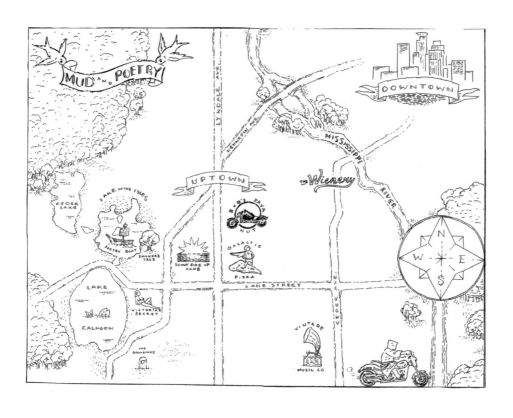

1

Mud & Poetry

We must not rank ourselves too low;
and with still greater care we must see that we do not
think of ourselves more highly than we ought to think.

—SAINT BERNARD OF CLAIRVAUX

Some people think of Christianity as the color white, like pure snow or vanilla ice cream. This might be why the occasional Christian takes all that is sexual and earthbound—with all of life's dirt and difficulty—and whitewashes it. Everything's bleached clean and bone-white and acceptable. But to me bleached Christianity offers a bloodless substitute for real life. I like to think of Christianity as a beautiful brown, like the color of Guinness or dark coffee. The kind of brown you find in the upholstery of seedy dive bars or of those working-class, brick-and-mortar haunts; brown like after-the-rain mud puddles kids love to jump in.

I think this because, as far as I can tell, at its heart Christianity isn't classy, and it isn't for prudes. Though it may well have inspired a lot of high-art and highbrow thought, it's also guilty of highballs and high heels. Christianity is true-to-life, which makes it chaste, yes, and holy; but it's equally sexually exciting and intoxicating.

For Christians, everything is compelling and sacred—everything except corruptions and inversions of real things. And this book explores what a single, Christian person like me finds compelling and sacred about sex, love, God, and everything in between. They're all related in the plainest yet most momentous ways. God builds his community here on earth, using ordinary, unsophisticated, soil-like mediums to give it shape—relevant to this little book's theme, the plain marriages of everyday men and women. It's unpretentious. It's sexual. It's lowborn and muddy. But it's alluringly holy.

o o o

And so I begin with dirt. If ever I marry, I would like to marry in a graveyard. In my daydreams, the ceremony takes place in the morning. The spring grass is wet with dew. Branches hang heavy with apple blossoms. My bride and I have two plots beneath a tombstone with our names and our Battle Cry chiseled above blank epitaphs. A string quartet plays at a distance while family and friends gather around our freshly dug graves. The priest reads from the 1662 Book of Common Prayer. There is no altar. There are no stained-glass windows. Over this austere monument and over these two yawning holes, we exchange vows (while a wedding reception is to be a drunk, merry thing, the wedding ceremony itself is to be a grave thing).

I am told the whole idea is morbid: to me, it's a beautiful and severe affirmation of the wedding vow—Till death do us part. In some degree, to marry is to say, "You and I will someday die." We cannot be together forever. Even if we died at exactly the same moment, we, like all lovers, would be torn apart, severed, "alone into the unknown."

God shapes Adam from the dust of the earth, and to the dust Adam returns. Marriage is a beginning pointed toward an end. For Christians, that end is God. One flesh. For a twinkling of an eye. And then, a six-by-three-foot flower bed.

This may be a morose way to start talking about sex and romance and marriage. But A Great Love is a serious thing. And only when we are serious—rightly serious about the right things—can we truly laugh and play. We begin with death so that we might live, and live well. You can't have poetry without mud. Christianity knows this. This is why, for all its Sistine Chapels and Dantes and Bachs, it remains the faith of messy ordinary people living messy ordinary lives.

But before I can tell you my story or talk about sex and love directly, I must start with mud and poetry. This first chapter describes and defines mud and poetry. It's tough to write about love and death without generalizations, and it's difficult to make generalizations without sounding glib. I am in many ways beyond my territory. I'm not married. I'm not a therapist. I'm just a house-painter bachelor with convictions and ideas. When it comes to marrying and making love and dying, I can only write as one comparing notes.

○   ○   ○

You can't talk about love without eventually talking about everything, because what love means depends on what the whole world means. Our idea of love hinges on our idea of life. The nature of love reaches back to the very first things, to our premises and presuppositions. I wasn't able to put words to love until I realized that what love is depends on what the human person is. And the human person is mud and poetry.

I cannot give you any definitive explanation as to why this is so: I can only stare open mouthed and point. For example, I am completely enchanted with the myth of Adam and Eve. Who wouldn't be? It is a story about a naked man and a naked woman; a story that takes place in a garden with apples and a snake and the possibility of immortality and doom, a myth of endless application and imagination. I do not mean myth in the abraded present-day meaning of "falsehood." To me human history is not only a sequence of empirical facts. Fact is essential, yes; but I'm also after the deeper wisdom and meaning of human experience; that is, the myth. Fact without myth is half the truth. But myth without fact is also half the truth. And so you will notice in this book that I often refer back to the mythic-factual story of Adam and Eve. It is a myth, but a myth is not (necessarily) less than a fact. I read about Adam and Eve, I read other books, I live a little, and I have this germinating hunch that humanity is made up of mud and poetry.

I remember reading about a study that compared orphans in institutions to children being raised in prison.[1] While the living conditions of the imprisoned children were hygienically inadequate, if not downright abysmal, the living conditions of the orphans were hygienically immaculate. Interestingly enough, the children raised in prison were far less susceptible to neuroses, illness, and even mortality than the orphaned children. The difference was that the orphans were raised by professional nurses while the imprisoned children were raised by their own (albeit imprisoned) biological mothers. Nurses, however well trained, perform their duties in a routine, institutionalized manner. Their primary concern is with physical need, with mud. Biological mothers, however, give natural affection, milk, and care. They are concerned not only with the physical health of the child, but with his heart and soul, with her name; that is, with poetry.[2]

The story of Adam and Eve has become a symbol for me. The way I see it, mud comprises the raw materials of life: water, shelter, food, sex, emotional need. Mud is, in part, needy biology. The "muddiness" of humanity is not a bad thing. We cannot escape it; we're not supposed to want to escape it. Mud is good. God formed Adam from the mud of the earth, stepped back, and said: "This is good—very good!" —Good, that is, mud and all.[3] Mud is the God-given, natural search for happiness and fulfillment in life. Mud is the stuff of which we're made: the hungry, dependent, mortal, finite goodness of being an emotional-spiritual-embodied creation.

The orphans had nutritious, clean mud. Yet they were more prone to neurosis, illness, and even death, than the children raised with their imprisoned mothers in bleak conditions. This is because the mud in humanity—the emotional, sexual, communal, *neediness* of human-ity—can't be met with mud alone. Bald existence cannot sustain a happy, healthy, fully human life. What the orphans were lacking was poetry.[4]

An upset baby reaches for his mother because a receptive and aware parent can soothe him; it cannot soothe itself. Mud cries out for poetry. A child cries out for caresses and milk and a name. And this need never goes away. Adults cry out for knowing and being known, for relationship, for affirmation, for connectedness and affirmation of that name. In the face of muddy death, the lover in grief cries out for immortality (the poetry in us defies death). We are inextricably both mud and poetry.

It's beautiful, really. God formed Adam from the mud of the earth and then lifted him up, rejoiced over him, and said: "It is good—*very good!*" And out of that joy and out of that approval he bent down and kissed Adam, breathed life into him—breathed poetry into him. That kiss confirms our place as creature in relationship to our Creator. In some unknowable yet obvious way, we bear God's image, his like-ness. This breath, this kiss, this pulsing, restless image-bearing, is the mud and poetry of us. We are more than a body. We are auras. God knit our spirits to our bodies seamlessly. We are emotional-spiritual-physical people of passion, fertility, heartache, bad cholesterol, bad ovaries, great art, and great relationships. The depths intermix with the heights. This is the joy and burden of being human. We are mud and we are poetry.

I think of poetry as what affirms and articulates our creativity, our scientific inquiry, our reaching outward and upward, our resemblance to God (and, thus, our amazing capacity to say to one another, even to God himself, "It is good—very good!"). Poetry is a soldier going to war for his county. It's a mother making breakfast for her thankless children. It's Rothko and Cézanne and Kavanagh and Milton. It's children playing on a playground. It's what happens when a man stammers to ask a pretty girl out bowling or to the movies. It's making love. It's taking Communion on Sunday morning. Poetry is when we call each other by name (and say, in so many words: "It is good that you exist!").

Christianity is God-lit and shining, but it's also a beautiful brown. And this is because real life is not only God-lit but also soil-like and messy. Mud and poetry are not so much binary as they are a spectrum.[5] A person isn't acting out of only either (a) pure poetry or (b) pure mud. Mud and poetry overlap and intermingle, sometimes so as to be indistinguishable, the wide spectrum of existence we call life. We cannot separate spiritual from physical, life from death, and (consequently) joy from pain, and even need from gift. But still, generally speaking, there are distinct differences between the two. While mud is the emotional-spiritual-physical neediness and ache of being human, poetry is "the sweetness of life"—the relational, celebratory, art-making, procreating, happiness of existence. Poetry too is emotional and physical and spiritual. But it is so in a way different than mud. Mud moans, and then it sighs. It takes: it eats, digests, takes comfort in. Poetry sings, and then it laughs. It offers: it affirms, celebrates, pushes, stretches out. In short, mud needs and receives; poetry gives and creates.

Think of a cup. We either come at each other empty, thirsty, and looking to be filled (mud); or we are full, full to overflowing (poetry). We are at one moment needy and dependent and at another bursting with love and creativity. Our life is rooted in mud. We reach up to the sun: we drink the rain. We flower. We sing and we work, we make love and we build houses and we raise children. We die. We are but mud and poetry. And, because I don't want to draw pictures of make-believe, fantastical conceptions of the world, poetry and mud have to be pointed toward death.

o o o

This next section is about death, and its relationship to mud and poetry. In the same way that you cannot write a book about love without writing about everything, you cannot write a book about love without writing a book about death. We live to die. This is not to say that death is our life's purpose, but that we are all, even now, heading toward our deaths. Every evening before you pull the curtains shut, you look upon the horizon line of your death. And every evening that horizon line shines brighter, closer. By the time you finish reading this chapter, you will be nearer to your death than you were before you started. The view has no comfort, no vocation, no raison d'être. Death does not fulfill life: it puts an ax to it. Death is a catastrophe.

In one sense, however, I think death is natural. In our present fallen state, death is often a welcome thing. The body tires, the will ebbs. We wear.

> They tell me I am going to die.
> Why don't I seem to care?
> My cup is full. Let it spill.[6]

But in another sense, there is nothing natural about death. I don't think we were meant to die. Mortality was not an original part of mud or poetry. Death is the consequence of sin.[7] In the beginning we were without sin: thus, we were without death. But because of our sin, mortality has infected poetry and mud like a disease. We have fallen from our original state. We have fallen far from the glory, we have sinned, and we must therefore die.

Sin and mortality infect mud and poetry in different ways. Mud dies with the separation of the soul from the body. But poetry dies with the separation of the soul from God.[8]

Mud's relationship to death is more passive than active. Sin broke the harmony between the mud of our bodies and the mud of the earth. Creation became hostile to humanity. Humanity became alien to creation. Because of sin, the mud of the earth is now constrained to "bondage to decay."[9] Mud is passive: because of sin, our bodies now get sick, bend and droop over time, whether we like it or not. We can't do anything about it. But sin does not make the mud in us inherently evil. We will always be muddy. Even in heaven we will be muddy. But we will not always be mortal.

It was not out of muddy need that Adam and Eve ate the forbidden fruit. Eden offered all the mud—and satisfaction of mud—that mud could possibly need. It was poetry that took and ate the apple. For poetry transcends mere need. Poetry is desire, and desire and need are not the same thing. More accurately, the poetry in us is will. And will is the creative power to decide on and initiate, to affirm and negate, to make. It was a poetic gesture to eat the forbidden fruit. It was an act of sheer will and desire. And in the eating, Adam and Eve acquired the knowledge of good and evil—a knowledge so profound God cast them out of the Garden lest they eat from the tree of eternal life and become "like one of us."[10] And this, I think, is why poetry is the more godlike: it seeks to know and to create and to will. And since the Fall, poetry now knows both good and evil. Poetry of this capacity is no small gift. It is no small thing to be able to will against death, or to embrace it, or to even have a word for it—"death." It is an enormous poetic power to be able to procreate, to paint a painting, to commit suicide, to murder. The poetry in us is what we choose to make of it. We can choose good or evil. We can affirm or we can deny. We can love or we can hate. And we can give a damn or we can choose to not give a damn. That is poetry.

Looked at from another angle, the poetic gesture of sin is also just mud turned on its head. Mud is concerned with the needs of the me, myself. Deformed and unruly mud separates the needy self from its natural connection to others and to poetry. It becomes autonomous and greedy. Corrupted mud is a corrupted love of the self. And its fruit is the poetic decision to decide what is good and evil for ourselves rather than trusting God's definition of good and evil.

Why does mud tend to invert and turn in on itself? Why has every Christian cried out with Paul, "Why do I do that which I do not want to do?"[11] This incessant tendency of mud to become a cancerous obsession with self, to choose sin, comes close to the idea of humans having a sinful nature.[12] Regardless of whether original sin is actually a part of our true nature (our nature being what God made us to be when he first created us: his own image-bearers) or not, it must be said that in a post-Adamic world no human except Jesus has been without sin, that every human has indeed sinned,[13] and that, therefore, despite all our advances in medicine, the mortality rate is still 100 percent.

Nevertheless, while mud bears death more passively, poetry wrestles, embraces, or fights against death actively. Mud is now resigned to our mortal condition. But poetry is in a constant tug-of-war with that condition. Sin sentences both mud and poetry to death: though the mud in us has little to say or do about it (our bodies die), the poetical has much to say about it. The poetry in us stretches out into eternity: by its very nature, it defies death. Our bodies get sick, bend and droop and wrinkle over time whether we like it or not. But our spirits, our poetry, can continue to flower, form, and reform, unto death. While our bodies eventually fall apart, our spirits do not have to wrinkle and tire. The poetry in us is what we make of it. And for poetry to be formed around the good, the true, and the beautiful, it must be harnessed to those shining virtues faith, hope, and love—which is to say, the person of Jesus Christ.

Where Christ is, life is. Life comes from God. Sin is turning away from God and, consequently, from life. Death, then, is a separation from life and from God. This does not mean God is separated from us,[14] but that we have separated ourselves from God.

The Christian hope is that, in Christ, death is not the final word, that after we die God will breathe new life into our mud and our poetry, and it will then be raised up without the sin-mortality it now bears.[15] We will be perfected to glory—the Bible says the very glory of God.[16]

Christ died that we might live.

Yet we die.

Death is not natural, and yet, at the same time, it is the most undeniable prospect in life. While death is said to be defeated by the cross of Christ, and its sting removed by his resurrection,[17] death is still immanent. Even as the apostle Paul looks forward to everlasting life with Christ, he anticipates his own death.[18] He knew the old verse: "The soul that sins shall die."[19]

But always there is God, the God who is over and above and around everything we are. God can be trusted. And because God can be trusted, his revelation can be trusted. And because his revelation can be trusted, so too can our reasoning and experience be trusted. And if our reasoning and experience can be trusted, so too can our deep poetical longings and desires be trusted. And what does the human person—poetry, mud, and all—long for most? I wonder if it's not the fulfillment of our mud and poetry, in God and in each other.

Because there is God, there is not death and only death, but also the possibility of hope, reconciliation, and grace. For the Christian, death goes hand in hand with resurrection, union, full relationship, immortality, endless creating and re-creating, deep meaning, joy, and unfathomable glory.

> Yet Lord, instruct us so to die,
> That all these dyings may be life in death.[20]

mud love and poetry love

Although love is not easy to define, it has an inherent architecture, an order that can be excavated from the essential qualities of what it means to be human. As I have said, humanity is mud and poetry. This is a crude reduction, admittedly: but sometimes it helps to unnaturally dissect and define in order to see the natural whole. This is, at least, I think, the case with love. If humanity is mud and poetry, it follows that in its simplest forms there are two kinds of love: Mud Love and Poetry Love.

Mud Love is a beautiful brown, earthy love. It's a love for pillows and blankets, a love for pizza and beer. Mud Love is love for our own sake. No one loves beer for its own sake; that is, no one wishes it the best, or the good. We love beer for our sake. If we were to wish it anything at all, it would be that it would be in our pint glasses so that we could enjoy it. Mud Love is a needy kind of love. It loves friends and family and the next-door neighbor because of fear of loneliness. It loves because it is lonely, hungry, and cold. Mud Love fulfills our impulse for completion, satiation, and fulfillment.

The premise of Mud Love is that our whole existence depends on being wanted and being loved. We usually think that a good love is void of self-interest, that to love out of a need that we might be loved in return is to have an ulterior motive. A good love, we think, has no ulterior motive. But, as C. S. Lewis has observed: "We are born helpless. As soon as we are fully conscious we discover loneliness. We need others physically, emotionally, intellectually; we need them if we are to know anything, even ourselves. . . . Our whole being by its very nature is one vast need."[21] Only God can fully love without being dependent on being loved in return. As humbling as it is to admit, our loves always grow out of poverty. It is a rare occurrence indeed— at times, maybe even a divine gift—to love without any thought to self. (For even in acts of charity, as we use the word today, we are delightfully conscious of our momentarily benevolent selves: how many "selfless" acts of love are really hidden forms of self-love? How many masquerades of charity have really turned out to be mere stubbornness or bravado?) Indeed, only when we know we are loved are we able to love without any thought to ourselves. This is okay. In the beginning God designed us as needy mud. And he immediately met this need in his affirmation, "It is good—very good!"—an affirmation he has repeated throughout all of history in the tireless pursuit of humankind. It is okay that we cannot—could never possibly—love God as intensely as he loves us. It's also okay that we need each other, could never possibly come at each other without some thought to ourselves. God made us that way.

A whole love cannot emerge *ex vacuo*: it grows out of the dynamic muddiness of being human. Mud Love is the soil of the soul, the only ground from which any other kind of love can take root and flower. This does not reduce all human loves to self-love. We are capable of loving, of adoring and beholding, without thought to self. But self-love is the starting point, an inescapable and good reference point.

Jesus, the only man to ever be equated with Love Itself, first meets the muddy needs of a person and then loves them with a poetic love, a love that looks upon those in need and says, "The kingdom of God is at hand!" (Or in other words, "I still find you good—*very* good! I still love you. I still rejoice over your existence!") Jesus first touches warm mud to the blind man's face; then he tells him of his generous, overflowing love. If Jesus had merely healed the man of his blindness it would have been a half-healing. This is because (God knows it) we need more than mud. Mud Love cannot satisfy the desires it arouses. We need to be loved in muddy ways and in poetical ways.

Poetry Love is a love that inspires people to write poetry. Poetry Love is a vision, a beholding. It is contemplative. It is more roving than grounded Mud Love. For example, Mud Love is a sexual love. Sex is often bound up in Poetry Love, but sexuality is not the same thing as Poetry Love. Sex is muddy. Mud Love understands that a man wakes up in the morning thirsty for water and sex. A man in Mud Love (at least, Mud Love in its most rudimentary form) wants to have sex with a woman because of his own physical need. But a man in Poetry Love (at least, Poetry Love in its most rudimentary form) wants to write a poem about the woman, to sit under some tree and to think about her in a general state of woolgathering and delight. Later, perhaps, it may desire union with the beloved, but it will come at sex in an entirely different way than Mud Love. Poetry Love is enamored with a person. It desires union out of adoration and celebration, not out of muddy need.

Not that muddiness is bad. It's just different. Mud wants to possess and be possessed, to have your clothes ripped off or to be clung to on a cold and lonely night. Mud wants orgasm. Poetry wants to gather and behold. It wants to draw a picture of the beloved naked. It wants to cherish and connect, to become a part of her in some way. Poetry wants ecstasy.

Poetry Love refines and cultivates our most primitive Mud Loving. Mud Love loves beer solely because it's good for us. But with Poetry Love it is possible to respect or admire something, to simply rejoice over the fact that something exists at all. When someone says, "I love Rachmaninoff's *Vespers*," it means something entirely different than, "I love beer." Saying that one loves the *Vespers* is not just saying that one loves to listen to the music. What it's saying is that Rachmaninoff accomplished something inherently good and masterful, something truly great and beautiful apart from the listener, something that deserves to be enjoyed. It's pure affirmation. It's Poetry Love. Poetry Love is an appreciative love. It creates, honors, marks, lifts up, rejoices over, makes merry, memorializes. It is a love that does not love something or someone solely because of what they do for us, but because they are in themselves worth loving.

Poetry Love is a reflection of the Creator's creative love because it says of the beloved, "It is good—very good that you exist!" The premise of Poetry Love is that, being made in the image of God, we can love with not only a fully human but also a godlike love. It has the power to turn our gaze away from self and upon another. Poetry Love can turn our love into something self-giving. Self-giving, it must be said, but not self-less. Love is never self-less. If we can love with a godlike love, it isn't that God loves through us (although he certainly can). We ourselves are the lovers. It is true that without Jesus we are incapable of loving with the best kind of love possible. Compared to God's abundant love for us, our love is scant. In his *On Loving God*, Saint Bernard goes so far as to say: "Our love is not a gift but a debt."[22] John writes, "We love because he first loved us."[23] But this is not to say we are merely conduits or channels of God's love. When we love, we—not Someone or Something else—do the loving. God made us as human beings, individual selves. This is the enormous gift God breathed into us: we ourselves are actually capable of loving, and loving well.

When I say there are two kinds of love I'm speaking in shorthand. There are no such things as actual "Mud Love" or actual "Poetry Love": there are, rather, mud and poetry dimensions (angles, nuances, wellsprings) to the experience of love. Like the mud and poetry of humanity, the idea of Mud Love and Poetry Love is not so much binary as it is a spectrum. On the far left we have sheer need and on the far right pure adoration. On one side we have sexual desire (perhaps something like *desiderium, appetitus, passio,* or *sexus*), and what Lewis has called "Need-love"; on the other side we have self-giving, godlike "Gift-love" (something like *caritas, agape*). In between we have the whole range of subtle affections and loves (*eros, storge, amor, affectio, philia, philadelphia, amicitia*).

Like the mud and poetry of being human, Mud Love and Poetry Love overlap and intertwine. You could have muddy poetry or poetical mud. This is seen, for example, in the joy between a lover and his beloved. The mud in the beloved wants to—needs to—be loved (the joy of being loved). At the same time the poetry in the lover turns his gaze onto the beloved in delighted, self-forgetting affirmation (the joy of loving). He cannot help but love her, and in doing so, fulfills her muddy need to be loved and wanted. Yet, in doing so, the lover finds, perhaps startlingly, that he likes to be needed in this way; indeed, he might find that he needs to be needed this way (the joy of being needed). Something about Poetry Love, he finds, is actually muddy.

To add to the mix, the beloved might notice that her lover finds muddy fulfillment in her needing him, and out of her own muddiness voice, almost poetically (that is, for his sake, and not for hers), her neediness for his love, which he so badly wants her to have (the joy of someone else's need). And this can go both ways, lover to beloved, beloved to lover. We love to want and to be wanted. We love to love and to be loved. We cannot help but need and want to be needed.

Love is something we do and something that happens to us. Love desires to possess and enjoy and to set free and surrender. How Mud Love and Poetry Love seem to contradict one another, and yet at the same time complement one another, will always remain a mystery. This is because love is a mystery. We are poetical mud and muddy poetry. And so are our loves.

It cannot be said enough that to love out of only Mud Love is to love immoderately. Mud Love without Poetry Love is self-seeking, self-indulging, self-gratifying, self-love. It's a mask, a romantic affectation, a means of getting what you want. If Mud Love does not flower into Poetry Love, it can be quickly emptied of its inherent goodness. Mud Love is not inherently utilitarian, but without Poetry Love it can quickly become utilitarian, even dehumanizing. If you know only how to Mud Love, you will never see the world through the prophetic, loving eye of the poetic lover. A person in Poetry Love can hate no one. The whole world has been baptized, made hale and new. I cannot help but think of the old bearded poet yawping from the rooftops. He's not just booming about the goodness of a particular woman, but about the goodness of the whole wide world. Poetry Love, at its highest, is a godlike love, and God's love is an affirmation, "It is good—very good!"

To love is fundamentally to affirm. It always overflows from the specific object of love to the whole of things. Poetry Love makes the whole world lovable. This breakthrough, this discovery of something new, can be something like the joy of participating in what physicists call an experience of "elegance." Everything around you becomes unexpectedly arresting, simple, rich, eternally complex: it takes on a certain form, an inner consistency. All of a sudden you find beauty in tomatoes, alleyways, and grocery store aisles. It was always there. It just took an affirmation to see it.

Love makes us who we are and who we will become. As creatures created by God, we need both the mud and the poetry in love in order to become what we were intended to be. This question is the premise behind all different motives of love: What is the human person meant to be?

my award-winning chili recipe

The Ran Ham is a booze-stocked hole-in-the-wall bowling alley in St. Paul, Minnesota. It's entirely discreet, entirely underground, and entirely outworn. Every year for the last thirty, my aunt and uncle have filled the Ran Ham with friends and beer for their annual Charles Chili Fest. Old friends and family spend weeks preparing secret homemade chili recipes to battle it out over blues, corn bread, and rotgut. There are as many awards as there are varieties of chilies: Most Like Your Mother's, Most Like Hormel, Candy Ass, Peppy, Most Curious Chili.

One year I concocted a white chili so full of cilantro, garlic, and secret ingredients it qualified more as a mystery stew than as chili con carne. I set it on the table next to all the other more beautiful chilies and corn breads and immediately lost any hope of victory. My sense of despair was heightened when I saw that the seasoned members of the Chili Fest had Crock-Pots; my mystery stew sat at room temperature in a modest plastic bowl. But I couldn't help goggling the shiny trophy with all the previous victors' names engraved on it. I wanted it.

When the last of the beer is drunk and the last bowling ball hurled down the old Ran Ham lanes, after we have all stuffed our bellies with every possible chili imaginable and after we've cast our secret votes, we gather around to learn who won which awards.

I was not surprised when I won "Most Curious Chili" (the most comical award); my chili was curious, to say the least. But as the more prestigious prizes were awarded, I was shocked to hear my name called for the first-place Candy Ass prize. I had won! Everyone cheered and whistled and wanted to touch my shiny trophy. Even though I don't even like trophies, I gobbled it all up. In some silly way, it affirmed me—as a cook, even as a person, a person worth taking notice of, if only for a night. It sounds childish, but I liked being publicly praised. I loved the fame, the glory of it all. I was proud.

It was early December, the season of Advent, a season of expectation, hope, longing, and joy which begins four Sundays before Christmas Day and lasts until Christmas Eve. I remember stepping outside with some friends for a smoke break and thinking about my trophy and my fame and all the waiting and hope of the liturgical season.

Interestingly enough, Christian theology professes that the final stage of salvation is *gloria*—fame, being publicly praised by God himself. Glory, it is said, is the fulfillment of our existence.

The New Testament is thick with references to Christ in glory.[24] This God who became a Man—the Creator who became *creatio*; who died and, having died, conquered death and sin and then rose again to life—this Jesus will live on in glory. Christ will be glorified. And through him, all believers will be glorified. The process of salvation and sanctification is a process of self-actualization. The more we become like Christ, the more we become ourselves. Every single person is God's bold and rich original idea. And God has made every single person to share life in glory with him. The apostle John says, "Beloved, we are God's children now; it does not yet appear what we shall be, but we know that when he appears we shall be like him, for we shall see him as he is."[25] God's glory is the believer's hope and final destination. The apostle Paul writes "I consider that the sufferings of this present time are not worth comparing with the glory about to be revealed to us." He also says, "This slight momentary affliction is preparing us for an eternal weight of glory beyond all measure."[26] Peter as well tells of glory: "When the chief Shepherd appears, you will receive the unfading crown of glory."[27]

Created by God and created for God, we must remember, with Bernard of Clairvaux, that "it is not of ourselves that we are what we are. Unless we know this thoroughly, either we shall not glory at all, or our glorying will be in vain."[28] Mud and poetry cry out for fulfillment in Christ.[29] We don't want to be homogeneous and boring. We want to stand out, to shine, to be inherently unique persons with our own tastes and skills and perspectives on life. And we want others to acknowledge this. It seems childish but it's true. This idea of fame—of desiring to be singled out, chosen, acknowledged—is in our blood. And perhaps this is one reason why Christ says we must be like children if we are to enter the kingdom of God. A child seeks recognition not out of pride or vanity, but out of beautiful, sloppy mud.

○ ○ ○

What love is depends on what the human person is. Humans are creatively made, affirmed, and loved by the artist Jesus Christ. Our whole existence hinges on this affirmation. The human person is mud and poetry, the very image of God. Sin has buckled and warped that image, tangled the good of mud and poetry with neuroses and vanity and mortality into a confusing knot. And so in our present state we must ask, What is the human person meant to be? I believe that, despite our sin, in Christ the answer remains: we are each a one-of-a-kind creation of deep pathos and unique personality destined for glory and relationship with God. Good love acknowledges and affirms the immutable and eternal in the beloved. And if the question "What is the human person meant to be?" is the premise behind our reasons for loving and shapes how we love, then the concepts of glory and death, sin and salvation, mud and poetry, are inseparable from the concept of love.

This is why I begin with dirt. This is why I want to get married in a graveyard. Marriage is a celebration of the whole personality—mud, poetry, mortality, and all—of your spouse, his or her creation, and his or her redemption. Good relationships are a union with another personal being. They defeat loneliness through sexual and intellectual and personal connection. But good lovers do not simply gaze into each other's eyes. Their gaze is on Christ.

The Christian posture toward the world is brown and steeped in muddy real life. In Christian marriage, we usher one another unto death. For the Christian, a good love is a love with a view toward death, toward the beloved's final resurrection and rest in Jesus, his or her future *gloria*. In this light, to learn how to love is to learn how to die.

This book is a collection of vignettes about the thoughts that wander through the mind of a sexually charged Christian single; thoughts that swirl and eddy rather than course straight. The chapters aren't necessarily sequential or logically related. A lot of this book is the outcome of conversations over coffee or lunch with close friends. A lot of it is influenced by the books I discovered at the new-and-used bookstore just down the street from my apartment. And a lot of it tells my story. I couldn't possibly describe Christianity from every possible angle. As I can presently write but one book, I can approach Christianity from but one angle: here, mud and poetry, sex and romance, singleness and marriage. This book is not much of an apologia. It is the vague musings, the mental pictures and hyperboles of a waxing mystic.

Love God. Date and have sex and get married. Drink beer and laugh. Pray. But not necessarily in that order. That is the distilled message of this book. God is wooing us, building something beautiful, and we can be a part of his activity on earth.

2

Savvy-Bachelor Sex

For Christ plays in ten thousand places,
Lovely in limbs, and lovely in eyes not his
To the Father through the features of men's faces.

—GERARD MANLEY HOPKINS

Any woman will do, just give her a bath and send her to a
dentist.

—LOUIS XVI

waiting for my elliott smith

I used to think I was the perfect boyfriend, but that was before I had a
girlfriend. In my youth I had enough virginity and books on courting
to build a tower to the nonhuman. The view from up there was good.
Gods were forged and girls swooned, particularly over the silver ring I
wore on my finger, which shone with all the brightness of chastity and
good intention. I was as green as an unripe banana.

I didn't have a real girlfriend until I was a sophomore in college. She was as shapely as a mermaid and loved Christ and cigarettes and good coffee—a powerful amalgamation—and all my stars seemed fixed in her orbit. Her name was Jess, and she was a post-pothead who had kissed a lot of boys. I was a nineteen-year-old prude who had smoked pot only once and had never kissed a girl; yet, for all this, she was gracious unto me. We kissed for the first time after a techno party. I had covered my face in an invisible paint that glowed under a black light, and after all the guests left, the paint slowly covered her lips and face. I thought kissing was like licking an ice-cream cone, which is probably why she kept laughing as she taught me what to do, and a lot of what not to do, with my awkward tongue and teeth and lips. At sunrise I walked Jess home, grateful and covered in glow paint, surprised by how different she looked outside the thrill of the ultraviolet light.

I hadn't planned it that way at all. I'm usually not one of the techno beat, black light, and glow paint ilk. But real life is never quite like what we map out beforehand, especially people; especially kisses.

High school girls often make lists outlining sought-after attributes of future husbands: short hair, lots of money, no tattoos or piercings, probably wearing pleated khakis. I don't like lists. Whether the tattoos or the money, I never seemed to make the cut; but that's not the only reason why I don't like the idea of making a list. Lists are too limiting. When you meet someone, wouldn't you want more than what you thought up yourself? If I actually met the woman of my dreams, I would meet nothing but the hardcover, feminine edition of my own imagination. I'd want to keep her, for sure, but as one might keep a collector's item—unopened and with the original dust jacket. It would be boring. I would rather be taken aback, surprised by how very different this woman is, not comforted by how perfectly she fits into my checklist.

Don't get me wrong. It's good to know what you like and what you don't like. Sometimes you just have to lay down the law: I'm sorry, I can't date you because you have a Bluetooth cell-phone earpiece stuck in your ear, you smoke, you sport a Calvin-peeing sticker, you don't look better when I drink, you drive a PT Cruiser, and so on. But still, as a general principle, I don't like the idea of the suitor-sweetheart checklist. It tends to close more doors than it opens.

I work part-time at a local coffee shop with a girl named Catherine. I love Catherine because she's a liberal and a vegetarian and because she's not afraid to disagree with me. She says she's waiting for her Elliott Smith (a singer who died under tragic circumstances in 2002). She listens to his albums all the time because his music speaks to her heart. This is beautiful. If for some reason I were to make a list of what I'm looking for in a spouse, it would begin with this: that she speaks to my heart, that I could carry her heart in my heart.

What I learned from my first kiss is that you have to listen. I sometimes wonder if love is the great iconoclast. True love rips apart whatever early images of perfection we might conjure. We can't project our grandiose plans onto others. What you have before you is a real person, not an idea. That first kiss probably looked like a program about a lion hunting on the Discovery Channel. After the long chase the lion is happy to chomp and shake its prey, oblivious to anything but its sated appetite. It wasn't until I learned to step back, to listen, to put aside my assumed familiarity and acknowledge how unfamiliar I actually was, that I began to learn how to kiss.

And, as far as I can tell, this is also the great secret to marriage and sex, and the whole of love.

○ ○ ○

It's easy to think ourselves good at loving until we actually experience love. We might have lofty ideas about courting, purity, and chivalry, but our relationships reveal who we really are. They are a standard. They judge us. Until we learn to put aside the pictures in our heads and love the actual person in front of us, we will never truly love.

Reading too many books about courting before I ever actually had a girlfriend put unrealistic ideas in my head about what a relationship with a woman is really like. And the same thing applies to sex.

Here I can speak only for adolescent men. When it comes to sex, we live in a fantasyland. If I were to write a book about young men's sex lives it would start with something like, "At the end of the day, when I'm lying alone in bed. . . ." I remember when my sister started bringing boys home for dinner. I warned her that every boy in high school is a sick, drooling thing, part monster (I was once one). Nonetheless, she liked the monsters. The problem with pornography and masturbation isn't only that it's lust, but that it builds towers to the nonhuman. You learn to love a knockoff of the real thing. You get too comfortable with yourself and your individualism. When you finally face a real person, you'll be shocked by how much is demanded of you, how much more difficult and vulnerable a real relationship and real sex can be.

Here's the thing. Reading Christian courting books isn't at all the same as pornography. But it had a similar result in me. I created a world of romance and sex and relationship that doesn't exist in real life. It was flowery. It looked pure. But it wasn't real. It wasn't a beautiful brown, like a pint of Guinness. And I believe relationships hurtle us, sometimes against our will, into the most fundamental reality of what it means to be human.

the tyranny of technique

Anyway, I dated Jess for about a year and a half. We had a lot of fun: we both liked the same bands, we loved the same kinds of beer, and we were both really into playing chess. We also loved kissing (which, looking back, probably didn't taste as good as I remember it because we were both avid smokers). We listened to a lot of Ben Harper and Kings of Convenience and Louis Armstrong. She loved Chopin and said she could play Chopin backward on the piano. To this day I think

I still have his Preludes somewhere. At first the relationship was a garden in bloom. Every day, more color and variety would unfold, and we would grow more in love. But there was no space in our togetherness, and we took too much too fast. Because of this, over time other plants crept into our garden, a garden whose beauty we thought would last forever, and crowded out what had been planted. I guess I just wasn't her Elliott Smith, and vice versa.

The interesting thing is that the farther our hearts drifted apart the closer we became physically. It was as if we were trying to make up for something, trying to warm our shivering hearts with the heat of our bodies. We had always been intimate, but now it transformed into a groping and clinging.

It was awful. The whole experience changed me.

I saw how love could not only make a person better, even bring them closer to God, but also how confused love, shades of love, can do just the opposite.

Confused love can become the closest thing to hate; confused desire, consumptive appetite, leading us to harm those to whom we intend good. For me, fear of isolation pushed the genuine desire for union and full relationship into unwarranted jealousy and exaggerated self-importance. The Jess I once loved became a threat. I become skeptical of her other friendships. I almost didn't want her to succeed. I wanted to be the center of her universe. I wanted her to depend on me, to fit into my plan. Love had wholly turned against itself.

The experience scared me. I was reading C. S. Lewis's *Screwtape Letters* around that time, in which Lewis wrote that for demons there is no difference between love and appetite. Love for demons is a literal eating of the beloved, absorbing his or her life into an extension of one's own, at the beloved's expense. Demonic love is a continually waxing hunger for a continually waning happiness. Love began as divine, singing like a god. But, as Lewis says, "when natural things look most divine, the demoniac is just round the corner."[1] I had already experienced the beginnings of how love can become an insatiable hunger and lovemaking little more than mutual masturbation. It was then that I learned a simple truth: love is not neutral ground. If we do not point our love toward the right end, we will only heap upon ourselves heartache and pain, if not worse. And I've been thinking about that for a long time, especially with regard to sex.

○ ○ ○

I've probably been thinking about sex for half my life. I was around twelve when the idea first took hold of me and now, at twenty-four, I still gawk.

Of course, to me this seems only natural. I am a young man. As I write this, it's springtime, Easter season, the season of Christ's resurrection, a season of light and life. Everything in my uptown Minneapolis neighborhood seems holy, hale, and new. Every nerve ending evinces a life of its own. Try as I might, I cannot suppress a feeling of duty. Like a soldier's commission, I feel like I am charged to accomplish a great and exhausting procreation. Abraham's seed fills the earth; Jacob loved Rachel; the salmon swim upstream to spawn and die, and so will I. But these primal abstractions are mostly my being poetical, melodramatic, and visionary.

I'm not exactly thinking about sex—at least the way most people use the word. Some people "do" sex like they "do" lunch, and see it stemming from the same animal appetite. It's all mud, fallen mud, and no poetry. In my opinion, sex of this sort declines in degrees from biological instinct to a mechanical and inhumane act. Pills, tackle, and textbooks clutter the bed beyond recognition. The headlines are multiple orgasms and simultaneous orgasm. And behind it all I sense a sadness. There is no truly happy "savvy bachelor." Read the magazines they read. They are good only at making money and entertaining themselves, and everything and everyone falls into one of these two categories. Sex becomes scientific; the how-to's of orgasm, suddenly paramount.

It's a tyranny of technique.

Playboy magazine epitomizes the savvy bachelor. He is charming and elegant, emotionally detached from the women he beds. After he rounds his fifth hour of intercourse, he makes a post-coital martini and goes to sleep next to a passed-out bunny. In the morning he is miffed that she wants to eat breakfast, talk, stay.

I don't want to be a sexual prude. But I wonder if by pretending that sex is emotionally and morally no-strings-attached, a person becomes an emotional prude. An emotional prude uses sex to escape the commitment and vulnerability required in genuine relationship. But when sex is severed from affection, marital jealousy, commitment, and the family, it becomes boring. Our savvy bachelor might have all the sex a person could hope for, but I imagine he or she is haunted. The heart cannot survive long when denied what it needs most. It breaks at the thought of inconsequence, of life and relationship without meaning—to have only mud, and no poetry. For all our tools and Kama sutra and sexual fitness, we have given up relational and spiritual intimacy. We do not look into each other's eyes. Again, look at the sexy magazines. Rollo May captures it: "You discover that they are not 'sexy' at all but that *Playboy* has only shifted the fig leaf from the genitals to the face."[2]

I believe God made sex interwoven with affection, the future, and death. Good sex is possible only in marriage. As far as I can tell, this ought to be a given. But a more subtle ingredient to good sex is buffoonery. My first kiss with Jess would have been a tedium were it not for our being able to laugh at all my unknowing. I can imagine little worse than a bed without laughter. And for this reason, I have long suspected that homely people and old people have the best sex. Old people, especially, who have worked down deep, and outclassed the inflated sex of youth. Their nuptial dance is not flaring like a peacock's parade, colored with vanity and pride. Their bed is humble and brave. Within the walls of fidelity and trust they are free to be truly playful.

This is not to say we shouldn't take each other seriously. We must be serious. Only by taking each other seriously are we free to romp and play. Sex, like food or wine, is one of the older jokes in the world.

It would be good to laugh again.

Sex can be sensuality, frolic, rejoicing, or lovemaking. But if we forget to laugh, it will never exceed mere sensuality. When taken out of the context of play, the kind of play only possible in trust, the kind of trust epitomized in marriage, sex becomes a matter of performance. The whole awkward-beautiful dance is turned into one big solemn production. We lose the natural grace possible only when we aren't aware that we're being watched.

Our savvy bachelor moves from one partner to the next, from one one-night stand to the other, a new body in his or her bed for every new phase of life. All are kissed in the same way, stroked in the same way, making no dividing line between one body and every other body. But when you line up a thousand naked bodies, the bodies become identical and identically meaningless. They become just one of the many in line. Neither lover has the right to shame ("to be naked and not ashamed" and having "the right to shame" are not the same thing). Savvy-bachelor sex fundamentally says your naked body is just like every other naked body. It's all fallen mud and no poetry.

In marriage, however, not all naked bodies are equal. Here, husband and wife come to each other to make their bodies extraordinary, irreplaceable, soul-full. In marriage we give the gift of positive shame (that is, guarding or covering what is worthy of honor or respect), the gift of pricelessness, one-of-a-kind-ness. We affirm both the mud and the poetry of being human. Writer John Updike looks over their three children to his wife of then seven years sitting on the living room floor: "You allow this black skirt to slide off your raised knees down your thighs, slide up your thighs in your body's absolute geography, so the parallel whiteness of their undersides is exposed to the fire's warmth and to my sight. . . . Seven years since I wed wide warm woman, white-thighed. Wooed and wed. Wife. A knife of a word that

for all its final bite did not end the wooing. To my wonderment."[3]
That's it. Absolute geography. As sacred as a sanctuary; as playful as
a playground.

There is no rumpus—hullabaloo, laughter, joy—in the savvy
bachelor's apartment. The emphasis on stamina, tricks, and secrets
is all part of the same tyranny of technique. The lovers might as well
be at a recital. Poor man and his phallic paranoia of size and stamina.
Poor woman and her obsessive concern with adequacy, the dramatized and seizure-like orgasm. When will we learn that the body is not
a machine, but a graying and wild-haired poet? That sex was never
meant to be performance, but poetry, with its own lilt and rhythm?
Saint Francis called his body Brother Ass, and laughed. He was the
merrier for it.

learning from the old and homely

I have just bought a record player because I'm tired of what headphones do to music. People jogging, people on the bus, people in the
hallways at school; everywhere we look people are listening to music
in their headphones. I think the listening experience that headphones
create segregates you from the other people around you. Although
headphones have a place and a time, even a definite value, instead of
bringing you closer to other people, iPods and MP3 players isolate the
listener. Historically, music has never done this.

With vinyl, however, you can't help but want to share music
with others. When guests visit, we pour the wine and flip through
the records, carefully open the covers and read lyrics, and we listen
to the whole album from beginning to end. We're brought together
over something we share, even if it's a disagreement about who rocks
more: the Beatles or the Rolling Stones? Brahms or Beethoven? The
Smashing Pumpkins or Pearl Jam? With vinyl you tend to really listen
to the music, not as background noise, but as something to be heard,
something to be discovered and rediscovered, something to be shared.

When I visit my grandparents we play cribbage. Papa and I will usually split a beer. We banter. Grammy usually wins the game, and then we turn up one of their favorite LPs—Bing Crosby or Frank Sinatra. And before we get through the first record, Grammy is swooped up in Papa's arms, dancing. They sing the songs they've sung a thousand times and dance the same steps they've danced for almost sixty years. I love visiting my grandparents. Their conversation is easygoing, soft in the simplest way, and sane. They're happy, practical, and they're real. And the music they listen to is more than background noise. It's part of what brings them together as a couple, something they gather around.

I think great art was never meant to be experienced in isolation. Art is complete in community, in the relationship between the artist and the critic, the viewer or the listener. The experience of great art is a discerning, enjoying, edifying, reception. And what is love but a creation of an art that brings two people together?

Drawn to its end, savvy-bachelor sex fundamentally says the partner has no value beyond being used. It's perverted Mud Love. Locker-room talk calls it screwing. It is an impoverished sex. To "get laid" is a softer phrase but equally insufficient. Here, mere sex is a dressed-up but ultimately diluted substitute for the sexual yearning that courses much deeper than biological lust.

We undress, but we are not naked.

Yet what we need most is to be naked—naked and not haughty, naked and not ashamed.

I don't want to think about my grandparents having sex, but in order to understand—appreciate, even—a sex unspoiled by all we crowd around it, we need to learn from the old couples. We need to learn how to listen. We need to go back to before we somehow let music isolate us from other people in the room. Go to the old couples. If they have piled up the years, stacked them high and strong like a monument; if they have learned to love after the thrill of being-in-love vanishes (love can't stay twenty-three forever; at some point, there comes a falling-out-of-love, a shedding of the old before the discovery of the new. Aren't the *happy old couples* the ones who after the inevitable falling out reached for something more difficult and higher?); if they have learned to love by painfully taking root in each other, growing their love into something patient and beautiful, perhaps then sex becomes for them something more than all we crowd around it.

No, when I say I'm thinking about sex I don't mean anything close to savvy-bachelor sex. I mean something more sloppy and more glorious, something far more difficult—the difficult weaving of Mud Love and Poetry Love. Savvy-bachelor sex treats a person like an appliance. In the words of writer Harvey Cox, a person becomes nothing but a *"Playboy* accessory."[4] Savvy-bachelor sex doesn't need a hurting, laughing, dreaming soul, but a receptacle, a device. It is sex without a face. *Playboy* is a hall of statues perfectly lifelike, but perfectly lifeless. God leads Ezekiel, and us, back and forth across a floor of bones and hallowed women, "Prophesy to the four winds, breathe breath into these slain, and they will live again!"[5] We can hear it now, murmuring—the divine spark in her.

Stop talking.

Step back, and be glad the world doesn't end with you.

A person's body is particular and set apart. His or her soul is individual and sacred. He or she is mud and he or she is poetry. To lie in bed with someone touches the edges of something vast and indefinable. Pablo Neruda felt it in his "Body of a Woman":

Body of my woman, I will persist in your grace.
My thirst, my boundless desire, my shifting road!
Dark river-beds where the eternal thirst flows
and weariness follows, and the infinite ache.[6]

what we are

When I asked my friend Stephen what I should call him in my book, he said, "Call me Stephen the Philistine." I laughed. Stephen the Philistine is a tall, ash-blond man with a fierce gaze. We go way back, and we have been through thick and thin together. I respect and love few men as much as Stephen.

The funny thing is, I actually can see why he's a Philistine. He's not a Philistine in the contemporary use of the word—an uncultured, tasteless swine. Stephen's probably the most educated, cultured friend I have. He's a Philistine in the old, Bible-story sense—a pagan, a disbeliever; a *Philistine*. Stephen's a Philistine because even though he knows the theology and history of Christianity, he just doesn't believe. He says you need more than information and proofs to have faith. He doesn't believe because he has never experienced God, never felt him the way so many Christians talk about feeling him. And he's right. Until you've actually been touched by God, felt his love for you, have known you're loved, Christianity will seem fishy. And so Stephen finds experience in what is actual and at hand: a good mint julep, a thick book, a great album, or women.

I don't blame him. In my less-pious moments, I'd confess that I too have a Philistine moving around in me; and (I like to think) when Stephen's not being such a stubborn sensualist and aesthete, he'd confess to Christ's moving around in him too, like a prowler just outside the door.

Anyway, we lived in a little yellow house we called The Bench, and it was fully furnished with a bar made out of an old bowling alley lane and a kegerator and a front porch for smoking. After Jess and I broke up, I became angry with God and with love and women and life in general. I would take out my anger by completely disregarding what I believed about God and sex and everything in between. I figured that I had invested in holiness and it had only let me down. If chastity didn't help make my dreams comes true, if my dream of A

Great Love could just wash away like a tiny sand castle despite all my years of chastity, than I wasn't going to put much stake in chastity.

It was great. My whole senior year of college we threw parties. One night things got so rowdy the cops came to break things up, and Stephen got arrested. With some animation he wouldn't let the police enter our little house and was eventually chased down, shoeless and without any cash, and thrown into the back of the police car. Hours later, we picked him up at the station, Stephen the Philistine and Hero. We brought a pair of shoes and just enough scrap change for bail. We then promptly called every one up for a second Bench party. We didn't sleep at all that night. The whole experience was invigorating.

I have never drunk or danced or smooched so much in all my life as I did that year; and yet I have never been so depressed.

Stephen says I'm the kind of guy who wishes he were sexually unbound and illicit but remains devoted to the chaste and the boring. I would like to think he's right, but I know better. I'm both. "Give me chastity and continence, but not yet!" says Augustine. I want the good and the bad. I want the kingdom of God and the Wide World. I think a lot of us experience this common tension. Christians come up with a lot of contradicting philosophies. I'm no exception. And I sometimes wonder if my whole sensualist escapade could have been avoided if I would have just drunk more coffee and read more of the Bible in prayer in the morning. The Bible is like an anchor, something solid, poetic.

I should add that, despite all the partying, God found me at the end of that year, but that's a story for later. I mention it now because when God found me again, I began to see people almost in the way I think God sees people. And it frightened me. That whole time my relationship with Jess was crumbling, when we were trying to make up for it physically, and the whole time after we broke up, when I was smooching girls, I thought I was only toying with sex. It wasn't until later that I realized I was toying with people, real people, the women I couldn't bring myself to look in the eye.

I don't think you need to have sex to figure out what's going on. I was cavalier with something that was never meant to be taken lightly. Real sex is rarely about sex. If sex at its worst moves the fig leaf to the eyes and denies the personality animating the body, I think good sex is bound up in the eyes. It's about more than an orgasm. It's about more than being in love. Indeed, I think it's about even more than procreation. Sex (within marriage, at least) is the intertwining of two people, a mixing of mud and poetry, two souls becoming one as God intended.

I wonder if a giving and a taking of this kind, of this incredible heaviness, carries eternal consequences. As far as I can tell, sex is often, and rightly, simple and plain—a warm blanket or a good laugh, a drink of water or a "nightcap" before bed. In many ways, sex is simply the embodiment of love. But no matter how plain or sensual, sex always touches a person—not a toy or a bunny, not an idea or an adventure, but a person.

And I believe this enormous fact, this person, shoves us—whether we like it or not—before the very face of God.

It was when God found me again that I realized the horror of sex. Every person—every, single, person—is a snapshot of God himself. Jesus Christ makes it so. "What you do to the least of these, you do to me," says Christ.[7] We are quick to apply these words to the homeless man on the street, the strangers in our lives. How much more, I wonder, should we apply them to our spouses? No one has seen the face of God and lived to tell the tale. If Christ's words are as real in the bedroom as they are on the street, then sex is beyond what we know.

○ ○ ○

In sex and love we stumble into the life and world of an-other. A person. Can you look him or her in the eye? The ideology of *Playboy* spreads, just under the surface, like a cancer, spoiling not only sex, but relationship, love itself. It can even hide behind phrases like "I love you because you are so (sexy, smart, useful, funny)," if the subtle implication is, ". . . as long as you are so (sexy, smart, etc.)." To borrow from Josef Pieper again, what the true lover says to the beloved is, "It is good that you exist; how wonderful that you are!"[8] She is beloved, not just because of her merits, but solely because she is. Ironically, given the way we behave, it seems we would almost prefer to be loved for our performance, beauty, or wit. Yet to be loved solely because we exist, because we are who we are, a personality all our own, is what we so desperately need.

No, I'm not thinking about mere sex. I am thinking about God and the month of April, and how ordinary, commonplace love affairs are far from incidental. They trickle into eternity. And how only once we realize this we will begin, only begin, to understand sexuality. And sexuality is about so much more than something we do: it's about who we are—mud, poetry, and all.

You are holding the story of my thoughts on sexuality, thoughts that took shape during my one-year experiment with celibacy. But in order to tell it, I had to first tell you about Jess and The Bench and what I think God's true opinion of us is. We are God's beloved, the ones he dreams about. He's the one who put the longing for A Great Love in our hearts. And this is the frightening thing I have learned: in love you are either facilitating the ravenous Ego of Hell or provisioning the beloved's unique personality for eternal glory. We are, here and now, swaying our neighbor for better or for worse, shaping to some degree the fabric of their forevers, preparing them for abiding joy or unending torment: to become, in C. S. Lewis's words, "immortal horrors or everlasting splendours."[9] We are not only what we seem to be. Even mailmen and hairstylists are potential gods and goddesses—or monsters and devils.

It was difficult to tell you about Jess and how my love grew into something scary; it was difficult to tell you about how I used women and alcohol to escape all the hurt inside me. But this story isn't so much about that. It's about how God loves us; about how he wants to draw us to him through every part of our lives—even our sex lives.

The activity of God is playing all around us, like beautiful music. We just have to learn how to listen.

3

Saving My Pennies for a Motorcycle

While you and i have lips and voices which
are for kissing and to sing with
who cares if some one-eyed son of a bitch
invents an instrument to measure Spring with?

—E. E. CUMMINGS

a vincent black shadow

Marriage and singleness, love and sexuality, how we see things—they are all connected. Love means something very different to a nihilist than to a Christian. Faith, science, poetry, and any other means of understanding reality shape how we love. What we think love is depends on what we think the whole world is.

Sometimes my friends and I go out for breakfast at the Sunnyside Up Café. It's just down the street from our apartment here on the south side of Minneapolis, and it's the tackiest greasy spoon in town. For some reason when we're there we end up bantering about starting a Band of Brigands. We would cruise the country on our bikes, stirring up trouble, wielding unorthodox weapons. Stephen says he'd be infamously known as the Destroyer of Cities. He's good at coming up with cool names. I can only think of dumb names, like Tyler the Criminal, or Tyler the Terrible. He also gets the 1950 Vincent Black Shadow. Since the cool bike's taken, I opt for the less glamorous but nonetheless sleek Honda Shadow Spirit. We usually end up arguing about what we would call our hypothetical biker gang, who would get the black leather jacket, the red handkerchief, and other such matters of import. We go home full of eggs, agitated, and dreaming of the open road.

Sometimes I feel guilty about wanting a motorcycle. In my mind it's something a savvy bachelor would own, one of his many diversions. I don't want to be the guy who gets a new toy every week, anything that will delay a responsible, familial life. But I can't help it. I want to feel the sun on my shoulders and the pavement beneath me. I want to feel the wind in my hair, to smell the world around me. But maybe it's more than a bachelor's dream. Maybe it's like the longing Saint Francis had for open fields, or Saint Benedict's dream of an ordered life around Christ. I think of the desert fathers and mothers retreating to desolate places to pray. I get itchy feet for these prayer spaces. I want to go out and see the world. I want to see it the way the mystics saw it, full of the activity of God.

○ ○ ○

How can I describe the way God moves through his world, holds it together? It's as if there is no law of gravity. For Christians, the whole world is magical. Or, if magical is too unsettling a word, Christians at least believe the world is miraculous; that is, they at least believe in miracles. And once you believe in miracles, things change. God shows up everywhere: in the garden plot my grandma sows every spring, in my friends' faces at the Sunnyside Up Café, in the purr of a Honda motor.

I think Christians need to take seriously the contributions of modern science. But we ought to do so in a particular context. We look at the world and try to understand what holds it all together. As Adam named animals, we name forces and recurrences. We try to grasp objectively what we perceive through scientific inquiry. But as soon as we name our observations, we betray our presupposed (often unscientific) assumptions about the world—whether we believe a human being is like a machine, or the world is like a clock, or the universe is like platonic circles and lights. Everyone has starting points, a place from which they see things.

For Christians, Christ is the only starting point. Jesus is the single sine qua non, the one absolute condition. He is Lord of all things, not just some things. Take the law of gravity, for example. There is gravitas. There is weight. Things fall. As to why, neither Newton nor Aristotle could say. There is only the Christ of God, the *Logos*, ringing through creation. Christ is why rocks fall.

This is, at least, the thought behind my motorcycle daydream. It's spiritual wanderlust. What is the one thing in life that is absolutely certain? The love of Christ. "Christ is the Center," as Bonhoeffer puts it.[1] "Christ is the circumference and the center," says Bonaventure.[2] The kingdom of God is closer than we think. And, because Christ is so present in our world, my longing for the open road is not just about a motorcycle. It's about getting out of the everyday humdrum so that I might better listen to the God who is there.

I know it's probably overly romantic, and I know a theory that could never be falsified is also, for the same reason, never really verified; and no one wants to live in a world of metaphysical and theological abstractions: but I am not out to prove anything. All I know is that Christians believe God once stopped the sun, Christ once calmed a storm, even walked on water, and that if we have even a coffee bean of faith, we will (so we're told) move mountains.

The world rings with God, smells of him.

When you house-sit, the strange smells and arrangements of the home are at first striking. And even though the longer you live there the more the place begins to bear your marks and share your smells, traces of the original owner remain. You open a closet or a box, and it all comes flooding back. In Genesis, Adam was asked to be the caretaker of creation. Humans have impacted creation ever since. But even though the world now bears our marks and shares our smells, it still carries the fragrance of the original Owner. I admit that every metaphor has a breaking point, but for me this is the best way to put it. There is no law of gravity. In some weird way, Christians believe God moves through the earth he made, as if he were behind every occurrence.

○ ○ ○

Psalm 14 says, "The fool says in his heart there is no God." Skeptics and cynics, according to the psalmist, do not not believe because of rational thought alone, though a good deal of brain work backs up their often-presupposed hypothesis. They do not believe because of a conviction of the heart. Now, it would be dangerous to make a poetical division of a person that couldn't lead to any other conclusion, regardless of how someone actually makes decisions, but this perspective nonetheless fascinates me. To reject God is not merely an intellectual decision. It's also a decision made in the heart. And the same is true for those who believe. Faith is not only a matter of intellectual nut-cracking. It's also a matter of the heart.

What is the language of the heart? While the language of the mind is proofs and systems, the language of the heart is pictures and poetry—Bach's cello suites and Michelangelo's frescoes, good stories, cheap wine, and kisses. You cannot rationally justify kisses. You kiss because of the heart. Christians often try to turn the poetry of Genesis 1 into a proof or system to fight against or to mesh with evolutionary theory. They try to make it something other than poetry. Genesis can be read literally. But I think it's a story, not a dissertation; and as such, we should read it as a story, a true story. I think that if science says humans are 98 percent the same as all other mammals, we shouldn't argue back with scant scientific evidence. Why not give them, as the Bible does, poetry? Tell them you know that, genetically, humans are mostly the same as any other mammal, but that your belief that we are not the same is not based on scientific or historic proofs, but because the Bible tells us God shaped a man from warm clay with his own two hands; because he bent down and kissed him.

God breathed his life into us.

I am not a human being because I have a vascular system; I am a human being because I have been kissed, and (Lord help me) I will give kisses!

And here's the thing: if you believe it when you say it, if you really believe it, however they might scoff, they will be moved, not in their heads, but in their hearts. The heart flutters when God speaks, even when he speaks from the most unexpected of places.

Stephen the Philistine doesn't need a good argument. He knows the arguments. What he needs is the experience of God. I sometimes wonder why Stephen—Stephen the Philistine, the Destroyer of Cities—and I are friends. Most of the time he drives me crazy. Sometimes I wonder if one of the only reasons we're friends is because we love to disagree with each other. He totally disagrees with my poetical synthesis. He says he's going to make a shirt that says, in capital letters, NO POETRY PLEASE. Sometimes I wish Stephen weren't such a big part of my life, that I had been married to a righteous babe instead of being his roommate for five years.

I believe the kingdom of God lives in pictures and poetry because these are the languages of the heart. Pictures cut to the heart. A good tattoo can do more to communicate God's way of salvation than the most articulate pamphlet of the street evangelist. Poetry cuts to the heart. As the great poet Czeslaw Milosz pens it:

Novels and essays serve but will not last.
One clear stanza can take more weight
Than a whole wagon of elaborate prose.[3]

What we have to work with is story, poetry pierced with meaning. To say there is no law of gravity is, admittedly, somewhat hyperbolic. It's not merely semantics, though: in my experience, very little is "merely semantics."

Christ still lives. He fills our daily world with meaning, vividness, and color. Christendom is not some extinct dinosaur, but a living embodiment of God's redemptive work and love. And theology is a reading, and appreciation for, the Christ of God, in whom all of life is deeply rooted.

I think theologians are like music critics. Some of them drain the explosion and beauty out of a work with their reviews. Others totally miss the artist's message. But critics and theologians have always been a mixed bag. They come and go. God is still the same. He still has much to say to us today, especially on matters of daily life, especially on love and sex. And, for all I know, he is what I feel in the wind on the Open Road, the real ache behind my black, shadowy motorcycle wanderlust. I believe you can experience God, feel him the way you feel the wind or the way you feel the force of gravity holding you to the ground. And the beautiful thing is, God wants us to experience him this way.

a vow of celibacy

There are many ways I could tell this story. I could clothe it in white so you'd think I'm a saint. I could iron out its wrinkles and fold it into something more suburban, the kind of faith story I imagine most people like to hear. If I were a different person, I could tell a different, more inspiring, and less quirky story. But the true story, the story that's not dressed up at all, that's just me in my boots and old blue jeans and Hanes cotton undershirt, the story that's me, is the only story worth telling—not because I'm saintly, but because I know God is in it, despite myself.

This is one of the things I like most about Christianity. Your life story no longer ends with you. It's swept up in God's story; and, consequently, it becomes the story it was meant to be. It's like the more your life becomes caught up in a story bigger than yours, in God's story, the more you become more fully yourself.

It rings like a platitude, but it's true: you need to lose yourself to find yourself. It's beautiful, really. And proportional.

For me the end of my college career, when God found me again, and when I moved back to Minneapolis, was a remodeling time. One November morning, about six months after I graduated, I woke up pretty down. Although my college days of too much beer and too much smooching, when I thought I could live life apart from God, had ended, it wasn't until that morning that I realized a couple of things. I started to see that I needed to change, to grow—especially in my sex life. It was as if God lifted a mirror to my heart for me to see all the idols I had there.

I lay there in bed, thinking. How did I get here? I realized that, spiritually, I had always had one idol, A Great Love. Deep down I dreamed of passion, lovemaking, domestic adventure, shared tasks, and visions. I can relate to Adam in the Genesis story. I am missing a rib. I ache. I am not whole without a complement and a counterpart—without Eve. From the beginning man has had a God-given longing for a woman, a friend and lover, a wife. But, like Adam, I had clouded the image and twisted the natural longing into something unrecognizable. If sin is the suspicion that God is withholding something, that things would be better if I took matters into my own hands (as Adam and Eve took the fruit), nowhere else is this more evident for me than in my romantic life, my sex life. In the red coals of my heart, I knew I had forged a god. Always and everywhere I had put A Great Love before God.

Physically, I had lost the meaning of sex. My attitude about sexuality had bent my heart on self-expansion and self-gratification, as if sex were entirely about me—and that glimpse of myself appalled me.

Emotionally, I had created a habit of heart that looked to Eve to fill a void only God can fill. Let's say I'm lonely or restless: I will phone a girl, or write her a letter; I'll date—anything but face head-on what I must do for God to complete his good work in me. And I knew I needed to do something about it. I knew something needed to change.

Eventually, I got out of bed and made a big pot of hot coffee. And that's when it hit me. As weird as it sounds, I knew I needed to take a vow of celibacy. I needed to cleanse my body, scrub the hell out of it. I needed to be made clean. I vowed to be celibate for one year. I somehow knew that for one year I needed to not smooch or masturbate or date or roll around in bed with a girl. I needed to not even consider dating. No romance. No looking to Eve to meet a need only God can meet. Nothing.

Whether I was going to be good at it is another story (a big part of the story). But for me, celibacy was the lonely path I needed to walk. I meant to deliberately put myself in a place for God to work in me.

Celibacy for a time might seem like an oxymoron. The vow of celibacy, especially clerical celibacy, is usually for a lifetime and unconditional. But phrases like "intentional singleness" and "holy bachelorhood" just wouldn't capture the geography of the journey I took. Celibacy implies inner solidarity with God and his kingdom. For me, celibacy is a prayer. And prayer, at its best, is life. It was for me a plea, first to grow in relationship with Christ, and second to redeem my relationality and sexuality. It was a vow of celibacy with a view toward marriage. Unless the lifeblood of Jesus courses through my veins, my love is not much more than noise, like the clanging sound of misshapen cymbals or of bad rock music. The only way I could see this happening was if I went back to the headwaters, to the wellspring of life. Only out of the superabundance of God's love and good intention for me, would I ever be able to be a good friend, lover, or husband.

Behind me trails a wreckage. And I am hungry for God.

What distinguishes celibacy from singleness is intentionality. I wanted to be single for God. I don't want to merely stumble through a series of haphazard relationships. To smash the god of A Great Love, I needed to completely close the door, even if just for a time, on even the possibility of romance. As long as romance remained a possibility, the carrot dangled. And so I took a vow of celibacy for one year.

I was scared. I sometimes panicked just thinking about it. But I had to do it. I saw no alternative.

○   ○   ○

I started small. Jesus told his disciples to fish for people. But in my situation, I wondered if he was calling me to fish for hours. What I do tonight, in this hour, is what I do with my whole life. For what is there to one's life if not the moment, the here and now? We have to spend our days. We can't save them up.

What I do now shapes what I will be tomorrow. What I do now is what I will do in marriage.

Sexual maturity doesn't happen overnight (unlike losing your virginity). So many young people seem to think that masturbation, pornography, anxiety, and insecurity will somehow vanish once they are married. But no one would apply this principle to any other part of life. Runners train before a marathon. A person hosting a dinner party plans the wine, entrée, and dessert beforehand. If I want to buy a motorcycle next summer, I need to start saving my pennies now. "Those who cross the sea," says Horace, "change their sky but not their soul." If I do not work to develop sexual maturity now, I will drag all the chaos into the marriage bed and into the life of an-other.

My marriage depends on my now.

I need to redeem the hours, the scattered moments of my days.

They will (by God's grace), become a patchwork of moments, a tapestry, a love story.

○ ○ ○

To give some embodiment to my resolve, I went to Saint Patrick's Guild, a shop in St. Paul, and bought a couple of icons. I brought them home and fashioned a prayer nook by my bed with candles and the Book of Common Prayer. Once, not long after my vow, I prayed the prayer of Thomas More by scribbling it over a sketch of the cross and hanging it over my bed. It looked etched, as if in pain. I need pictures as a way to bring color and meaning to my life.

I also had my good friend Damien mail me a scapular to wear around my neck. Damien and I are the kind of friends who don't need to speak. When we were in college, if we had something to say to each other, we would just arm-wrestle or sing folk songs around the campfire or light up our tobacco pipes after dinner. Damien can drink more beer and recite more poetry with more vim and vigor than anyone I know. He can also do more push-ups than five of my friends combined. We became friends when we learned that we both believed trees had souls. To me Damien is a saint. And, even though he's now also a Marine, he's a mystic through and through.

Anyway, I wrote to Damien and asked him to send me a scapular. A scapular (from the old Latin word scapula, which means, simply, "shoulder") is a religious pendant with two signs that Christians sometimes wear. Monks and nuns wear these necklaces around their necks as a sign of devotion or as a reminder to seek Christ and to love the lost.

There are two signs on a scapular, one that hangs over your chest and one that hangs down your back. The bands that hold the signs, called the *jugum Christi*, rest on your shoulders and represent the yoke of Christ, "taking up your cross." The part that hangs over your heart, called the *scutum*, represents the shield, the "breastplate of righteousness." Christ before me; Christ behind me. I think that because we are a people who need rich symbol and imagery, outward signs of inward graces, and because there is a romance and a natural good to "binding God's law around your neck,"[4] scapulars are a good reminder of our baptism and the cross of Christ. Scripture verses that come to mind are "Let the word of Christ dwell in you richly," and, "Let not steadfast love and faithfulness forsake you; bind them around your neck; write them on the tablet of your heart."[5] Wearing a scapular was a daily reminder to pray, to turn my sexual energy into enthusiasm for God.

Although admittedly a weird idea, for me taking a vow of celibacy was the only natural thing to do. I didn't want to make the same mistakes I had made with Jess again. I needed to become intentional with my sexuality. And besides, the idea just felt right. I needed a different approach. (Whenever I think about monasticism I think of Giotto's fresco of Saint Francis of Assisi preaching to the birds. You have to think of the world a little differently to start preaching to birds.)

Ever since I was a child, I have glorified the monk: robed in itchy russet, standing in his solitude, passing his days in silence; living with the brothers, baking bread, working with his hands; singing the morning lauds and evening vespers. To me, a monk is like a biker. He is a man of fierce solidarity in Christ. To him God is like gravity. He perceives the whole of his life entirely in terms of a journey, a journey toward Christ. We need monasteries. They are a living dialogue for the church, a lighthouse for the traveler.

In my mind monasticism is one of the best models for living. Perhaps ironically, it's also one of the best inspirations for Christian marriage. Monks band together. They lean upon one another's strengths in areas where they are themselves weak. They build sanctuaries and hermitages. They build community houses and schedules around God. Some monastic orders mark time not by days, months, and years, but by the seasons of the church. I love it that, in this light, Saint

Benedict saw the abbot's chief work to be the *opus Dei*, the work of God. Monks endeavor to grow holy together through intentional living. And it all weaves a pattern, a healing and transforming rhythm for life. So also should Christian marriage.

motorcycles, minivans, and spiritual transformation

Our culture is unwinding the good bonds of marriage. We need to recover what celibacy teaches us about sex and marriage. I think one of the reasons why so many of us don't see marriage as an explicit Christian way of living is because we do not understand celibacy. Christendom has always been fiercely for celibacy and fiercely for Christian marriage, "kept them side by side," says G. K. Chesterton, "like two strong colours, red and white."[6]

For the Christian, celibacy and marriage complement each other. Monks and priests understand celibacy, often explicitly expressed as a "mystical espousal" to Christ, from the picture of marriage. And our forebears learned of godly marriage from celibate priests and monks. And here is why: celibacy captures the depth of human longing. The prayer of Augustine describes our longing well: "For thou hast made us for thyself and our hearts are restless until they rest in thee." I also like this quotation attributed to Blaise Pascal: "There is a God-shaped vacuum in the heart of every man which cannot be filled by any created thing, but only by God, the Creator, made known through Jesus."[7] We are hungry for God, and we can't help it.

But our longing is also for an-other. Everyone has a sex life, even if they're not having sex, even if they're monks, because we were designed to be sexual creatures. We are mud. Monks understand that the sex drive is more than animal attraction. For we are also poetry. This longing is like a compass, and it's not just pointing to the opposite sex. It also points to God. Sexuality is about more than sex, just as marriage is about more than you and your spouse: in the context of Christian marriage, sex is heavy with the possibility of revealing God's deep purpose for your life.

As I said, sometimes I think of monks as bikers. I imagine a bearded, tattooed, solitary man riding on a Harley into his unknown tomorrows. He's happy to be single, happy to pursue his solo calling, content with his sparse lifestyle. A family man drives a minivan or a Volvo, but a biker rides solo. He finds God on the freeways and in the garages, feels God in the physics of his bike on the road.

As simplistic as it sounds, until you are married you are single, like a biker. Even when you start dating someone, you're still single. You need to remember that until your girlfriend or boyfriend is married, she or he is also single. And when a person is single, she or he belongs to Christ. Don't make a claim on somebody to whom you have no claim. True love is never in a hurry. A good love is an unrushed love. While I am single I am called to Christ and Christ alone, before any Volvo or minivan, before any summer romance or Great Love.

Both Christian marriage and sexuality must be understood by the same principle of celibacy: every Christian is called to Christ and is restless until united with his or her Lord. The Christian life is a journey toward Christ, toward wholeness. Celibacy and Christian marriage anticipate what John envisioned all the saints someday shouting: "Hallelujah! For the Lord our God, the Almighty, reigns. Let us rejoice and be glad and give the glory to Him, for the marriage of the Lamb has come and His bride has made herself ready."[8] Whether we have been aware of it or not, everything inside us is bent on union with God. And outside God's generous heart there is no deeply fulfilling love.

Humans were made for Christ. Only out of this wellspring of love can we ever hope to transcend the natural human tendency of burrowing inward and to experience the joy of knowing others intimately. Marriage, then, if it is Christian, ought to assist and encourage the heart's longing for God. "Love must, in every sense," says Charles Williams, "be about [the] Father's business."[9] Like celibacy, Christian marriage should be concerned with the beloved's heart becoming a closer rendering of Christ's heart. Our final vision and enjoyment of God will replace earthly marriage. The church will outlive this world; your spouse's love for the Lord will outlive his or her love of anything on this earth, even his or her marriage to you.

o o o

When participating in the activity of God there are only two paths toward Christ: celibacy or Christian marriage. All Christians have for their destination Christ, and your options for transportation are (so to speak) either a minivan or a motorcycle. Either you can be married or you can be deliberately single for Christ. And this is because your baptism marked your death to the world. You no longer live for yourself. Condos and toys and aloneness are closed to us. There is no savvy-bachelor option. You must reorient your life around Jesus. And where is Christ more present than in your neighbor? Before he is found in books and sermons, Jesus is found in community. Both marriage and celibacy can be a training ground for sanctification, for learning to love as Christ loved us. Neither is better than the other. It's just that while one is the pursuit of Christ through mystical espousal to Christ, the other is the pursuit of Christ through marriage. No Christian is just a Christian. Before we are husbands and wives, as celibacy knows, we are Christians. Yet our task is not merely to be Christians, but to be Christian husbands and wives, Christian fathers and mothers, Christian siblings or children. You must join yourself either to a spouse or to a mission, to a monastery or to a community. Our job is to dive into the heart of Christ by diving into the lives of others.

One thing Christ showed us when he became human was that ordinary life is the raw material for building the kingdom of God. And what I was looking for when I took my vow of celibacy was something more than a tidying up of things. I wanted to be changed, completely renovated.

The idea isn't novel. Christians call this process of renovation "spiritual transformation," the movement and growth of the whole person toward Christ: Christ in the interior life; Christ in our interactions with others; Christ in the spiritual disciplines (prayer, fasting, worship, Bible study). As Paul urges: "Do not conform any longer to the pattern of this world, but be transformed by the renewing of your mind. Then you will be able to test and approve what God's will is—his good, pleasing and perfect will."[10] Or again: "We, who with unveiled faces all reflect the Lord's glory, are being transformed into his likeness with ever-increasing glory, which comes from the Lord."[11]

The idea behind spiritual transformation is that, in Christ, we become like Christ. Because of the grace of the gospel of God and the activity of the Holy Spirit, we can embark on a lifelong process to become more like Christ. This kind of transformation always involves the whole of life. It gives form to the Christian life. And this is something I want desperately. I want a life in Christ where Christ ties together every loose thread of my varied interests and responsibilities into a single whole.

It wasn't so much because I doubted whether I'm called to marry or not to marry. I like the way Kierkegaard puts it, and I agree with him: "Marriage is and remains the most important voyage of discovery a human being undertakes."[12] As far as I can tell being single, Christian marriage is an at-hand way to manifest God's kingdom here on earth in a practical way.

Christ wants to capture every part of ordinary life and redeem it.

He wants us to delight in what he has always been: the beginning and the end, the center and the circumference, our first and everything. And marriage can be a window into the personality of God.

Savvy-bachelor sex is easy. Building a relationship, a relationship that demands our whole attention and enhances and broadens the lives of both partners, is very difficult. Celibacy is not a condition, but a daily decision. Marriage too is not a condition, but a daily decision; not a fact, but a daily act. Genuine in-loveness is not what romance stories make it out to be: a summer romance, an exciting affair, usually not serious or lasting. Such stories present an exaggerated, sentimental, or idealized picture of love. We often equate "romantic" love with feelings of excitement, mystery, or passion, often in the context of a random or irrational relationship. Unfortunately, today's ideology values this kind of romantic love more than any other dimension of marriage, even practicality and prudence. For some, falling out of love is justifiable grounds for divorce. But if the idea that falling out of love justifies ending a marriage is spurious, and it is, then the idea that falling in love justifies beginning one is spurious as well. I will talk more about this in the chapter "Crazy Love."

Given the unrealistic picture of love made popular by romance stories, when it comes to love many people today are sex-crazed, high-strung romanticizers, or cynics. (Stephen the Philistine says he's all three!) But Christ wants to give us more in our relationships. God's most important plan for your sex life isn't just to make you happy but also to make you healthy and holy. Ephesians states that God's master plan is to bring all things together in him.[13] This is beautiful. Christ wants to gather our messy humanness and wash it, make it new. God has given a divine pattern for sex and marriage in scripture and history. Even more, our marriages can give us a picture of God's powerful courtship, of how he calls his imperfect but beloved church his own. Christian marriage can be a school of spiritual transformation.

If I had to capture what I'm after with a word, I would call it romance. Romance is what my motorcycle daydream and vow of celibacy are all about. Romance is what spiritual transformation is all about, especially in marriage. At its heart Christian marriage is an inner movement toward God. It starts with the heart, and moves out through the hands and eyes into a broken and waiting world.

God wants to redeem every part of daily life.

Nothing is overlooked.

Everything matters.

In this way, I imagine that the Christian life is a lot like the experience a child might have when running through sheets and sweaters swaying from the clothesline in an afternoon breeze. To him, the variety of smells and colors strung together are not just distinct bits of laundry; they are an enchanted tunnel leading home.

4

The Wienery

When the moon rises and women in flowery dresses are
    strolling,
I am struck by their eyes, eyelashes,
and the whole arrangement of the world.
It seems to me that from such a strong mutual attraction
the ultimate truth should issue at last.

—CZESLAW MILOSZ

planning a wedding

It's a perfect spring Saturday in Minneapolis, and my friend James
and I are eating lunch at the Wienery. Even though we're sitting on
old-school, malt-shop stools, it still feels more like we're in a machine
shop than an eatery. Everything here is either stainless steel or beat-
to-hell laminate. You almost expect to see a swimsuit calendar hanging proudly behind the grill. (There isn't one.) A huge swordfish and
a deer's head with antlers are mounted on the far wall. It's not as

if anyone's looking, though. In this cozy, clean, and stalwart hole-in-the-wall, the regulars come from all walks of life: pauperized students, luckless locals, and senior executives all line up around the same bar; order the best dogs and sandwiches in town (all for less than five bucks); and consider their waistlines as they deliberate spending the extra buck for piping-hot, house-cut fries.

We lucked ourselves onto stools by the window. It's a bright day, and all of this—the crowded grill, the smell of wieners and coffee, the mismatched chairs—has mollycoddled me into a state of complete repose. Maybe it's because wieners and an ill-assorted crowd are the perfect cure to a Friday night out. Maybe it's because I'm a sucker for cheap, delicious, metallic coffee. Maybe this is what James had in mind when he brought me here today.

"I'm going to marry Margaret," he says, completely out of the blue. I scramble to finish chewing while my mind scavenges for reference points. The last time we talked about Margaret, about three months ago, he was thinking about breaking up with her. I have no idea what to say.

"Hey!" I say, smiling, trying to hide my surprise with excitement. I look at him.

"Yeah," he says simply, looking at his dog and fries with a glow of almost embarrassed delight. I can tell he's happy.

"That's great, James," I say. "How long ago did you realize you wanted to marry her, that she was the one?"

"About two weeks ago," he says. And for the first round of dogs, we talk fondly of Margaret, and I mostly listen as James shares his plans for the forthcoming months.

Margaret really is amazing. She's smart, and pretty, and she's just crazy about James. I don't want to ask him what I'm about to ask him. I'd rather just look out the window at the people on Cedar Avenue and listen, happy in my ignorance.

"James, do you mind if I ask you a question?"

"Shoot," he says, and squirts the ketchup on his second wiener.

"I don't want this to come across the wrong way at all—I'm really excited for you, I am—but the last time we talked about Margaret you were wondering if you guys needed to be apart for a while." James nods as he buttons up his flannel. I venture on, nervous: "It's just that you guys were sleeping together—sleeping together a lot, actually; and fighting too. It sounded like you needed some space to get back on track, stop doing what you knew you didn't want to be doing. What's up? Why the sudden change?"

He looks at me. His answer is simple.

"I've already made a promise with my body, Tyler," he says, "and we love each other. She's amazing. I want to follow through with what I've started."

"Ah," I say in affirmation.

Who could ever fully know the deep-down heart of another person? Who could gather its fragments and sort out its varied hopes and heartaches, its joys, as one might organize a stamp collection? To me, his answer doesn't feel like the best reason to get married; but then, I don't like the idea of needing reasons to get married. It is brave and dangerous to venture out on someone like venturing on a ledge. To take such a leap, one must trust his or her own taste and discernment, judgment, and self-awareness. And before anyone can know whether another is right for marriage, they must first know something of what marriage means and demands. A boy who hankers after sex has no idea what sex is. A girl who yearns for marriage yearns for something she knows nothing about. Sometimes I wonder if marriage is something people just do instinctively. No matter how much (or little) we think about it, we marry. We can't help it. We can't help it, even though we learn in retrospect that we really had no clue what we were doing, that we were more caught up in an idea or running from loneliness.

"If, when I am drunk or sentimental or prodded by a stupid friend," says writer Mark Helprin, "I think back to the women I have really loved, most of them are covered and hidden by wishes and disappointment."[1]

I am also reminded of a passage I recently read by Robert Capon: "We marry on attack or rebound. We come at each other for an assortment of pretty thin and transitory reasons."[2] And as far as I'm concerned, when two people love each other and decide to marry, the rest of the world can either applaud or stand silent. It doesn't need to understand. What they have is theirs—theirs and no one else's.

We lay down our tip (a collection of wrinkled ones) and head out to where I'm parked. From there we go down to the Vintage Music Company, a record shoppe (it really is a shoppe). It doesn't look like much from the outside: just a nondescript brick building on the corner of Cedar Avenue and East Thirty-eighth Street. But enter the doors and you've entered a reservoir of musical wealth, a place where, if you're like me and don't know what you're looking for, you rarely buy anything. They use ambiguous genres like "pre- and postwar vocal and jazz," and the fastidiously categorized 78s are arranged by serial number and packaged in faceless brown sleeves. Boxes and crates crowded with records litter the floor. I like it here because when you enter, you are immediately overwhelmed by the musty smell of aged paper and sleek vinyl. I also like the bronze busts of Beethoven and Mozart and the gramophone horns.

Coming here today with James, I couldn't help but think about how this little music shoppe is like marriage: if you don't know what you're looking for before you enter, you'll quickly get overwhelmed. You might even give up. It's not a place for window-shoppers. It's for serious music collectors, only those who really care, who really want to listen.

Today we leave the Vintage Music Company empty-handed. Back at my apartment we listen to familiar favorites like Patty Griffin and Mark Kozelek and Modest Mouse and drink the cheap beer I keep in my fridge for lazy Saturdays just like today. I love Patty Griffin. Her voice is like a weapon, a scalpel to my heart. She is the great lyricist of our time. We drink Pabst Blue Ribbon, listen to music, and don't talk much more on this tall, blue afternoon.

○ ○ ○

Sometimes people ask me why I think I can write a book about marriage when I've never been married. Some older friends of mine have asked me if I'm too young to write this book. They say I'm a spring chicken. I haven't lived enough. It's true that youth rarely sees around the corner, what's just beyond the horizon line. It has no lessons for it has not earned them. Youth has only convictions. And most young people's convictions are blind and absurd and the dreams of "children ardent for some desperate glory."[3] Perhaps, then, this is why I must write this book and write it now. Only at this time of my life can I love with the blind hope of the virgin, one who has not yet played at "Hiding the Skeleton" or seen "Love's corpse-light shine."[4]

I don't think James's marrying at twenty-two is a bad idea, although one can argue that it's inherently better to wait to get married. When lovers marry young, the folk song that is their lives is still in its opening bars. They can write it together, exchange lines and melodies, add or abridge verses more or less ad lib. If they meet when they are older, their songs are more nearly complete compositions. They have not become somebody together. Every note and every refrain means something different to each of them. Either way—marrying young or marrying older—has its benefits and mishaps. We sing our folk song into the silence, hoping for a musical answering. And what joy—what attacking, indescribable, easing joy—when someone sings back! Generally speaking, I think the idea that we must "experience life" before we are mature enough to marry is based on false premises. Why not become somebody—experience life, travel, mature—with the one you're going to spend the rest of your days with?

Nonetheless, it's times like these, when I talk to James about his sex life and his new excitement for marriage, that I realize how important it is to think about these things beforehand. Experience isn't at the center of what makes someone more or less ready to marry, and the fact that we're comfortable with young people marrying proves the point. The fact is, you've been single your whole life and when you marry all that's going to change. No amount of experience will train you for what it's like to share a bed and a bathroom and a checkbook with the opposite sex. But I suspect caring about the right things—having the right convictions and vision for your marriage—can go a long way.

Experience doesn't preserve the marriage. The vision is enough. It will be a lifeboat when the going gets rough. What is the marriage vow if not an affirmation of the vision? The vision gives content to the vow. One of my favorite poets, E. E. Cummings, says it:

> you shall above all things be glad and young.
> For if you're young, whatever life you wear
>
> it will become you; and if you are glad
> whatever's living will yourself become.[5]

I think that since young people can marry, then young people can, and should, have radical vision for their sex lives and their marriages. "Those who wish to succeed," scribbles Aristotle, "must ask the right preliminary questions." When we are old and tattooed we will have stories to tell. Today we have only poetry and chivalry and causes, good intentions, rough drafts of the real thing. I think this is enough, though; more than enough.

What I do now shapes what I will be tomorrow. And so, in some weird way, even though I'm single, I am living my marriage now. And that's exactly what this book is about—what singleness can teach us about sex and marriage, and what sex and marriage can teach us about the kingdom of God.

the when and where of miracles

It is now Eastertide, a seven-week season after Easter (including Ascension Sunday) of continued celebration of the Resurrection and its implications. And here I am, writing about things that are way over my head. Perhaps I ought to be spending my time on something within my reach—like how to grow herbs in my backyard garden, or learning yoga, maybe reading *The New Yorker* or a Betty Crocker cookbook: anything but sex, God, and marriage; anything but how they're all connected. I'm not a theologian. I'm not a pastor. I'm not even churchy. And when it comes to sex and relationships, I'm definitely not an expert. But then, whenever a man kisses a woman, no matter who he is, he's in way over his head. And when you're baptized into the kingdom of God, no matter how good or informed you are, you're in way over your head. And writers (at least the better ones) have always been lost in clouds way up over their heads. So I'm not really doing anything new here. I'm just scratching my head, trying to make sense of spirituality and sexuality, trying to wrap my mind around the miracle-ness of it all.

A few years ago I copied this passage from a love story I was reading at the time into my journal: "Our love . . . seemed to us a miracle. First love always does, the old, old story sung by the poets and sneered at by the wrinkled of heart. And yet it is a miracle, an unbelievable miracle. . . . Here and now, in us and around us, the glory."[6]

The idea that love is a miracle can be easily dismissed as lovers' talk or mere sentimentalism. I have even heard Christians question the existence of miracles. I have also seen Christians walk out of church on December mornings, when the snow clings to the branches of trees and red cardinals fill the world with birdsong, and not pause to look around. They hurry to their Fords in families of four or five and turn on the heat and the radio, hardly aware of each other, oblivious to the way the light seems to move slower, thicker, and brighter on Sundays. To look is not always to see; and to listen is not always to hear. Most people don't know the difference.

Maybe this is why men look at pornography and why women read romance novels.

Maybe this is why the divorce rate is so high.

What if romantic love (and marriage) is about what we assume it's about? I wonder if we're missing something in our relationships and in our sex lives, the way the light moves slower, thicker, brighter.

The Bible says Jesus healed withered limbs and filled blind eyes with sight. He even raised the dead to life. I grew up in the city and saw relatively little of the natural world. But when I was young, I watched my mother take iris bulbs, soiled and seemingly lifeless, and plant them in the ground in straight rows, like tiny dead men. Every spring those bulbs take root and grow, become irises, and reach toward the sun. Every spring color and life again fill the gray garden in our backyard. And the irises multiply. In following years my mom would have to uproot dozens of the beautiful flowers to keep them from spreading into our yard.

We haven't seen a dead man raised to life for over two thousand years. We see irises spring up a thousand times every year. Who can say which is the true miracle? By what law do we discern which follows the natural order of things? We must remember that for the Christian, there is no law of gravity. There is only Christ, and there are the seasons, and what is to us a thousand years is to him but a day. When he walked our earth, he revealed God as a being of joy, a God who sings. And if God has given the earth the secret of how to receive a dead seed and turn it into a living flower, who can say he does not work the same miracle in the heart of a human being, even a heart seemingly dead?

Which is easier: for a doctor to mend a broken leg or for a therapist to heal the heart of someone who has been abused? If Christ has wrought in your heart new life in him, have you not beheld a great miracle? And who can say he doesn't give the heart of one person the secret to breathe life into the heart of another, even a heart seemingly soiled and lifeless? Does it not happen every day?

And does it not then break out, multiply a hundred times over? For all we know, we are God's miracle workers and we don't even know it.

Men and women, like my friends James and Margaret, have discovered each other for thousands of years. There have been thousands of kisses, thousands of hosannas, and hundreds of thousands of wedding nights. Ever since Adam first saw Eve, humankind has been gasping, At last! This is bone of my bone and flesh of my flesh! The primary reason we assume we know what it's all about is because of its almost universal familiarity.

When it comes to sex and marriage, pastors, psychologists, and gynecologists have made it all out to be something more quantifiable and technical than it really is. Maybe what women really need is to put down their books on psychology and sexology, to buy some pretty underwear, and to travel around southern Spain, maybe even to move there and open a café. Maybe what men really need is to put down their Playboys and books on Christian courtship and to backpack the Rockies or write poetry, maybe even to go on long prayer walks. Maybe they need to hash things out over dogs and coffee at the Wienery. I don't know. William Blake once wrote: "The naked woman's body is a portion of eternity too great for the eye of man," and I know right now it's too great, too eminent, for me.

I am like an unplowed field. My heart is close-packed and hard from wounds of past relationships and mistakes in my sex life. My mind is overgrown with lionized ideas about the way love works and what it's all about. Savvy-bachelor sex and Crazy Love have muddled things. And I've been missing something.

the songs god sings

You see, here is the secret every Christian knows but somehow forgets, the real-world fact no one can seem to get their heads around: God's long-term plan is to gather everything and everyone together in him, and he sometimes uses seemingly the most unspiritual means to go about it: sex and marriage, ordinary humanness. God's light has broken into our sin-darkened world and has been spreading out, and will keep spreading out, like a sunrise, until the whole world lives in the light of day. But the sad thing is, most of us think we're too holy for this aspect of it! It's too coarse, too sensual, too lowborn, too down-and-out human to be of God. "Can anything good come out of Nazareth?"[7] We'd rather have our church programs and our intellectual frameworks, our high stacks of books on chastity. At least in those we can escape the incredible difficulty of the here and now: the wife in your bed; the children waiting for dinner; your lack of a boyfriend; your annoying roommate; your unabated, clobbering sex drive.

But God wants to put back together what has been torn apart in our sin-wrecked sex lives. We read in Genesis that men and women are spiritually, emotionally, and physically fashioned to live in a God-imagined life of shared joy. Jesus has gone to work. He works still. He travels far and wide, establishing his kingdom from heaven to earth and back again. And his master plan is to bring everything and everyone back together again in him.[8]

God has come into the world to make his home among us, to make a home for us. And we can be a part of this great fight against humanity's spiritual homelessness. Every detail of our lives furnishes (or not) the household of God. In this way, Christian living is the great school of hospitality, of learning to make warm and loving spaces in a lonely and sin-cold world. And our sex lives are one of the most important places to start cleaning up in making things ready for God.

Christian marriage is God's garden. Regardless of whether James can say exactly why he wants to marry Margaret, in marrying her he is planting himself in a soil where God can grow something beautiful. Marriage can be a lot like baptism or the Lord's Supper. It can be a unique place where James and Margaret can meet God in a unique way. It can be a place where God can work in them and through them in profound ways. The activity of God is playing all around us, like a beautiful music, God's music. They can become a part of that music, a part of that song. And if Christianity is right, God himself is always singing. And maybe the fact that almost every song on the radio is about romantic love, that romantic love needs to be sung, is telling us something about him.

5

Who's Got a Scar?

In a flash, at a trumpet crash,
I am all at once what Christ is, since he was what I am, and
This Jack, joke, poor potsherd, patch, matchwood, immortal
   diamond,
Is immortal diamond.

—GERARD MANLEY HOPKINS

the couch society

Explaining all the good reasons that I took a vow of celibacy also means I need to describe my failures. I don't know what I was thinking when I took that vow. Maybe I thought that just the aura of monasticism would be enough to make me holy and chaste. Maybe I thought

Some of the behaviors and opinions mentioned in this book might be troublesome to some readers. The publisher does not endorse or condone behaviors that can be injurious to one's physical or emotional wellbeing, and trusts that readers will seek professional counsel when necessary.

that the bigger the plan, the better I'd be at following through with it. Maybe I thought that I would come out a saint. But in the end, despite all the brilliance of my plan, I didn't become saintly at all.

But before I can tell you that part of the story, I need to go further back, back to just after I had broken up with Jess and still thought I could live my life without God. That spring I went to study abroad in Oxford, England. Oxford haunted me. I have never been surrounded by so much grandeur and beauty; and yet, I had never been so alone. I believe beauty is meant to be shared, which seems especially true when you're in England. The beauty of that place pounded on my temples and in my eardrums, and there was no one to talk to about it, no one to share it with.

I have this same experience every time I cross the Atlantic Ocean. In fact, I have sworn that I will never visit Europe again without a wife—or at least a lover. When I was in high school, my family and I traveled to England, France, and Spain. I nearly died. It wasn't that I didn't love it there in Europe, or even that I didn't love my family. I do: they are, well, like family to me, a part of who I am. It's just that I simply feel attacked by all the beauty and the history and the deep meaning that seems to drip from every tree and reflect off every building. I get overwhelmed. Eventually, I get depressed.

I was in France, in the summer between my sophomore and junior years of high school, when I read John Eldredge and Brent Curtis's *The Sacred Romance*. It ruined me in the best way. My parents have a picture of me looking out over Paris from our hotel room—melancholic, thinking about God and sex and how lonely I was—with my brother and sister on each side, hugging me, confused by my mood. That book put to words what I had never been able to articulate. Even to this day, because of my travels through France with Eldredge and Curtis as a kid, romance is for me a holy word, like all those other robust words, words like glory or majesty or hosanna.

Years later, the summer after college, as a graduation gift, my dad took me to Italy to study Dante. We followed Dante's path of exile through some of the most beautiful places I have ever seen. It was amazing. I hardly studied Dante at all. The food and the women and the cities and the artery-like roads that meandered through vineyards were just too interesting. But for all the beauty and the good company of my father, I was bombarded with the most acute sense of my aloneness. All I could think about was Jesus and my fragmented prayer life. And lingerie. And how badly I wanted to spill my guts to a woman, listen and talk all day until we collapsed and I could fall asleep in her white arms. As ungrateful as it sounds, I did not want to be lying across a hotel room from my dad getting into bed in his underwear, talking about maps and architecture—a would-be perfect companion were it not for my hopeless romanticism and sex drive. I can't stand it. I'm never going back to Europe without a wife again. For me Europe isn't meant to be experienced alone. Traveling is just better when filled with sex and conversation and shared experiences of beauty and adventure.

So I found myself in Oxford, single and missing Jess, so overcome with longing for wholeness and relationship that I drowned my sorrows with a bottle. Within weeks after arriving I had gained a reputation for always having a bottle of wine in my hand. When I wasn't walking the High Street or studying in the Bodleian Library, I desired nothing more than to be a barfly. I also had insomnia, and for this reason it was in Oxford that I first began to write books. I would stay up late to write and to listen to all the bells from all the steeples.

But I failed miserably in my attempts to become an alcoholic. No matter how earnestly I tried, I just couldn't get drunk enough or depressed enough or angry enough to forget about Jesus. Joy always snuck in the back door, ruining my dramatic moods and making me happy. It was as if God wouldn't allow me to pretend that I didn't know I was loved and known by him, that I was actually well off. Jesus never let go, no matter how foolishly I tried to tear myself free. And though it took until the very end of my senior year of college, he eventually recaptured me.

○ ○ ○

The weirdest thing about Christian spirituality is how unspiritual it is. When I read the Bible, I am struck by how Jesus is never two-dimensional. He never speaks from some feathery realm. He never tries to outdo our world. Instead, he redeems it—what is here and now—and redefines it in himself, in his incarnate life and message and the whole redemptive process he set in motion in Mary's womb. The same Jesus who commanded us to poke out our eyeballs and cut off our hands was also accused of being a winebibber and a glutton. This probably means he glutted and bibbed a bit. To some the story of the wedding at Cana strikes an unexpected chord, coming from the celibate, supposedly ascetic Messiah. Jesus doesn't storm through the doors wielding a scourge of whips and overturning tables. He doesn't just sit idly, either. He turns water into wine. And by turning water into wine, it's as if he blesses and affirms the whole humanness of it all. Before Jesus heals lepers, before he restores the sight to the blind or loves the loveless, he participates in—of all things—a wedding feast. Ironically, Jesus inaugurates his ministry to save a broken and hurting humanity by affirming and celebrating humanity at its heart: marriage, wine, friends, a good party.

Anyway, God didn't call me out into the desert like I thought he would. I never rode off into the sunset on the motorcycle of my dreams, to fast and pray in Arizona or Utah. Instead, he surprised me by showing up at, of all places, the college parties we threw in our little yellow house, The Bench. I had at that time found myself to be the keeper of eleven bottles of booze, a full fridge of beer, two cartons of cigarettes, and against all this, a few eggs, an unopened Bible, and only a few dollars to my name. I had no idea that in the midst of so much brown—brown bourbon, brown whiskey, and brown days—I was about to be refreshed. It's as if God was tired of being left out, tired of seeing so much life wasted in praise of nothing at all. And he used, as he always does, the real, ordinary people of ordinary life.

At this time, Christianity had become incredibly abstract for me. I was happy to drink and smooch on Friday nights and go to church on Sunday mornings. And so, even though my heart was far from God, I started a theological discussion group. We eventually called ourselves the Couch Society, because we were always sitting on couches. We only had two rules: (1) No girls allowed. Girls would only change the tenor of the conversation and distract us. We figured we would end up wanting to impress them with our brilliance and wit instead of really hashing out the ideas in the books we were reading. (2) You must drink beer. Beer and theology just seem to go hand in hand. To talk theology without beer is like tinkering in a wood shop without beer. The two just belong together. The smell of sawdust and the sound of hammers call for a cold one, no more or no less, than the smell of books and the sound of male laughter call for a case of ales. Beer was essential.

At first nothing happened other than plain talk about theology. We talked about the tradition and Transubstantiation and postmodernism, and it was all very abstract and distanced from real life. But soon we began ordering pizza after our meetings. And we brought more beer and stayed late into the night singing songs and wrestling and talking. We listened to a lot of the Clancy Brothers, Luke Kelly, and the Wicked Tinkers. We loved singing old Irish drinking songs. Soon we were having slumber parties, sleeping over at one another's houses. Before long, we weren't interested only in getting drunk or smooching girls. We wanted something more. Though we couldn't articulate it yet, God was calling us to himself, through one another.

We wanted to take the Eucharist together. I think this is what happens when the Holy Spirit starts grumbling, like a bear waking after a long winter. I think when two or three are gathered together to talk theology, they just get it in their heads that they need to take the Eucharist. And so eventually, after the beers and the pizza and the evening's debates were finished, we would clear the living room for the Eucharist. We lit candles, sometimes we'd play monastic chant in the background, and one of our professors, Dr. Breyers, who is also a priest, would come by to officiate.

Dr. Breyers is a man full of laughter and wisdom, cracking a joke one minute, glaring at you from under his tweed newsboy hat and demanding that you repent and be saved the next. I love all things tweed and loafer, anything that suggests scholarship. I love how Dr. Breyers is always quoting Bultmann and Barth, or reminding us of Martin Luther's earthiness. He loves earthiness, especially dirt, which he swept out from under our puritan carpets. He announces large, sweeping faux pas in class. He tells jokes that would make Gandhi sign up for boxing lessons. You stop taking notes. The homeschooled girl's cheeks grow warm with embarrassment. Catholics are glad he's a Protestant. Protestants wish he were Catholic. But, even more so, if you're lucky, he'll invite you to his comfortable, stone house, where you can sit in his study by the wood-burning stove (one of four), look at all his books, and listen to the crackle of the fire. If you're really lucky, he'll take the picture of his wife from the mantel and pass it around, telling tales of love and devotion.

Right now is as good a time as any to tell you that, ever since I was a kid, I've wanted to be an Anglican priest. Growing up I read, over and over again, Jan Karon's Mitford series. They're no great works of literature, but I fell in love with the bachelor rector, Father Tim, and his life in Mitford, a small town located in wooded foothills. If I could have been anyone, it would have been Father Tim. I love how he's always quoting scripture or gardening, reading Wordsworth or working on his sermons. I love his sofa-sized dog and his chewed-up, favorite pair of slippers. I love the way he learns to become comfortable with his unexpected and unsought affection for his neighbor, the blonde and shapely Cynthia. And I love how Father Tim genuinely loves and serves the people of his parish. His whole life is like a tiny picture of what it means to be Christ in this world, no matter how plain or commonplace. This is one of the reasons why I love Dr. Breyers so much.

Dr. Breyers would come to our door bearing a small box, a Book of Common Prayer, and a head full of sermons. Wisps of his pipe smoke would fill our home, and I loved him for it. After we'd banter and smoke our pipes till the room was thick with smoke and stories, he would quiet us by opening that tiny box and pulling out tiny cups for wine and a tin of bread crumbs. We would pray. We would also worship. Sometimes we would set aside my bedroom as a makeshift confession booth for private confession before the service. Those were my favorite nights.

On a typical evening, empty beer bottles cover the coffee table. Couches are pulled close around. I'm expounding on how I want a Christianity that doesn't internally contradict itself: for example, the Roman Catholic theology of absolution of sins is, in my view, contradictory to the simple, plain talk of Jesus forgiving sins—and somebody speaking ex cathedra won't make it more true. Our doctrines and practices should not contradict the Bible.

Bryce, a Roman Catholic, tells me that the Catholic Church gave me the Bible, and begins drawing up logical, historical arguments in the vocabulary of Thomas Aquinas, his voice cracking and warbling the more excited he gets. I announce that I'm going to smash Bible verses over Bryce's head.

I'm thumbing through the New Testament. Peter has pizza all over his face. He shouts from a low love seat that Bryce is full of shit. Bryce retorts that Peter is full of pizza.

Stephen the Philistine's opinion is that we're all a bunch of overly educated virgins: "None of you knows what the hell you're talking about," he yells. And just before we all pounce on Stephen, the doorbell rings. It's Dr. Breyers.

Although Stephen the Philistine was a member of the Couch Society, he wouldn't take the Eucharist because he doesn't believe. Dr. Breyers nonetheless invites him every time to repent and be saved, to join us in taking the body and blood of Jesus. I remember one night when Stephen was particularly tired of Dr. Breyers's sermons and went to hide up on the roof of The Bench to smoke cigarettes and talk on his cell phone. When Breyers heard he was hiding, he delayed the Holy Eucharist and went out into the yard. It reminded me of the time when Jesus called up to little Zacchaeus in the sycamore tree. I remember Breyers standing there in our front lawn, thumbs hooked through his suspenders, glasses and fuzzy white beard, perfectly plump, looking up at Stephen and calling him down from up there to eat with us. I think God will get Stephen some day. Some day Stephen the Philistine will come down from his perch and eat and drink with all the company of heaven. (And that will be a glad dinner, to be sure.)

The whole affair was unassuming and humble in every way, almost tacky. But God found me there in the midst of all the pipe smoking and camaraderie, and it was like being welcomed home after a long absence.

the big dipper and a switchblade

I can't tell you the exact moment I was saved. I know when I said the sinner's prayer, and I know when I joined my first church, and I know when I was baptized in water. But the grounding moment in the story of my salvation wasn't any of these. It wasn't when I was baptized with water that I knew I was loved and known by God and meant for him forever. Instead, it was when I was branded with a switchblade.

To tell my whole story, I have to tell about the campfire and the stars and the switchblade, no matter how hyper-masculine or foolish it might sound. Some of the guys in the Couch Society lived at a house called The Styx, named after the mythic river in Greek mythology one crosses into Hades. The Styx was just out of town, on a farm surrounded by dark woods and open fields. The parties there were just as loud and lost as those at The Bench; actually, they were probably louder.

Things had changed for most of us members of the Couch Society. We were tired of sitting on the fence, not fully embracing the kingdom of God or the wide world. And we were hungry for God. We didn't want to live in sin anymore—not because we were plagued with guilt, but because we had lost the taste for it. It just didn't taste as sweet as holiness. Our newfound friendship was uplifting. Even though we were each a horrible mess by ourselves, because of Jesus we communicated Christ to each other.

One night we threw a party at The Styx. We burned a couch, drank cheap beer, listened to a friend play the bagpipes, and mingled. After most of the guests had left, around four in the morning, we gathered around the fire to do something that we hadn't planned beforehand. Each took his turn kneeling before the blaze, shirtless and cold in the early spring air, while the rest gathered around to hold him and pray. As one read a prayer from the Book of Common Prayer or a psalm, another held a switchblade in the fire until it was hot; and, with every friend close by praying, the glowing switchblade was then pressed into his shoulder.

Seven of us bear that mark. It stands as a testament to our frailty and the grace of God. The Bible verse that comes to mind is from Isaiah: "He was wounded for our transgressions; he was crushed for our iniquities; upon him was the chastisement that brought us peace, and with his stripes we are healed."[1] As my good friend John puts it, that night the scar on his heart was covered over by the scar on his shoulder, the stripe of Christ. That night was like a second baptism, a prayer. It was mud and poetry.

I know it's extreme, even stupid. None of it made any sense. But that's what we did. And for me it was one of the most important moments in my spiritual life. I remember clenching my teeth and fists, not struggling against the thought of any physical pain, but struggling against myself. Did I believe? Did I? Really?

I remember when I was baptized. Relief and gratitude washed over me when the flow of cool water enfolded me and buried me, before I was raised up into the warmth of the sun. I remember the profound change I felt within myself when I knew that Jesus was the

Christ, the Son of the living God. Neither death, nor life, nor angels, nor principalities, nor things present, nor things to come, nor powers, nor height, nor depth, nor any other created thing, will ever be able to separate me from the love of God, which rests in Jesus, the Lord.[2] I felt cleansed. I felt whole. Blood rushed through my veins with new life, newfound purpose. Sudden. Unfathomable. Perfect joy. That's what happened all over again by the fire with the Couch Society. It was a confirmation of the salvation Christ has already accomplished. I remember laughing and lifting my eyes to the night sky. "Is it really this candid?" I remember asking. "I believe."

Later that night we all camped out under the stars in a huge field. I remember looking up at the sky and thinking about how I do not understand many things. I do not understand the stars, though I wish I did. But I have always thought of the Big Dipper as a sign of a covenant, like the rainbow. Jesus asks the Samaritan woman at the well, and me, to "go and get your husband,"[3] knowing full well we have no husband, only middling lovers, only shams of the real thing. And then he invites us to dip our cups into the well, the only well in a dry land, filled with the only water that will really satisfy our thirst. And I'm thirsty. I want to drink until overflowing, until Jesus and his persistent love flow out of me into everyone I know. The Big Dipper. Drink God. The more you drink, the more you will be made whole.

○ ○ ○

As I write this, it's been almost two years since that prayer by the campfire. The Couch Society is scattered. We have all gone off into the world to make our livings. But God is as present to me now as he was that night. I think it's true that we human beings are buckled and broken because of our sin. It's also probably true that this simple fact is a clue to the meaning of our existence. So many of us exhaust ourselves in a lifetime of pursuits and dreams that will not satisfy us in the end. We want to be richer, more lovable, thinner, happier.

But I think this desire for wholeness, for something more, does more than suggest the meaning of the universe. It positively shouts it. God has put longing in our hearts, and, though we don't understand it, it haunts us. Even more, we not only want to be made whole, but we want to celebrate something, to worship something, anything. And I think this is a window into our souls. For me, the night we burned the couch and prayed together in the last dark hour before sunrise was when the windows and the doors of my heart were flung open. And I didn't know the world could smell so good.

failures

Even during the first month of my voluntary celibacy, I could feel God changing me in good ways. I remember how much I wanted to pray, and how peaceful it was to kneel at my makeshift altar in the evenings, looking into the eyes of Jesus on my favorite icon, Christ the Pantocrator (the Greek translation of "El Shaddai," applied by Christians to Jesus), the Teacher. I could feel my heart soften toward him, slowly; and I had never felt so at peace. I thought I was finally on the road to real holiness.

But it was only a little after this first month of celibacy that I not only committed one of the old sins, the familiar ones I was used to, but stumbled into new, uncharted wilderness. Through a series of circumstances, I kissed a woman. Twice, on two separate nights. What makes the matter all the more deplorable, even despicable, is that she was going through a divorce. Sure, she was practically an unmarried woman (she'd been separated for months because her husband was physically and verbally abusive), but I couldn't get over the fact that she was legally married. The whole experience felt adulterous to me; in fact, I think it was adulterous. And what's worse is that I had broken my newfound resolution to be holy in my sex life.

I was scared. Before this, my mistakes had felt mildly innocent. But not only had I broken my resolution to be holy in my sex life, for the first time I had also come close to committing one of those sins the Bible cries out against from beginning to end. I couldn't look in the mirror for about a week. One night I locked myself in my room, ridden with guilt—not only about what I had just done, but about so many memories of things I had done that I thought I had forgotten— and I was so ashamed, and so thirsty for God, that I burned myself on my arm with a pewter cross. I deliberately wouldn't let it heal for weeks. It was as if I needed the pain to relocate, change addresses, move it from my heart to my body.

Looking back, the way I handled the whole situation was not healthy. I was trying to cope with my emotions by injuring myself. I should have immediately run to Jesus, like Mary Magdalene, and grabbed his feet and covered them in tears. Sadly, it wasn't until another month later, when I confessed to the Couch Society what I had done and prayed with some of them about it, that I could acknowledge that Christ could forgive me; and indeed, already had forgiven me.

My confession came at a time when we were on a writers' retreat at a cabin in the north woods of Wisconsin. It was January, thick with snow, just a few days after Epiphany. It was Ordinary Time, the time from January 7 to the day before Ash Wednesday, a time when there is no unusual focus. Almost the whole Couch Society was able to make it, and we had brought enough beer and bacon and whiskey and books for a small army. All day we would write and go for hikes and smoke pipes on the front porch. And at night we would gather around the fire to read aloud one of our poems or essays, get lost in raillery or badinage, and nurse our tumblers, happy to be inside and warm with all the snow outside, seemingly worlds away. There, in that small log cabin, I realized that the reason I sin is because I do not trust God.

I think all sin is at root chronic doubt born of the fear that God is holding something back, that the old tree of the knowledge of good and evil in the Genesis story was intended to restrict our happiness rather than protect it. Doubting God, I take matters into my own hands and eat the fruit I know will not satisfy.

I seem to have a knack for this. But doubting God sets off a horrible chain reaction of events: first comes separation from God; then comes separation from each other; and finally comes death and eternal separation from God. It breaks my heart that so many of us think we need to obey God in order to avoid punishment, as if we could win our way into heaven. Rather than receive the superabundance of God's generous heart and in return love and trust him, we choose to live with a false religion and a Jesus that don't exist in real life.

But I don't think we need to climb to heaven.

Heaven has come down to us.

Jesus brought romance to our front doors. He is standing there, knocking. We need only open the door and invite him in. For all you know, he'll like your record collection and the paintings hung on your living room wall. Maybe he'll even bring table wine. Jesus has broken through the barriers and invaded our space. Like the temple curtain, the heavens have been torn apart, not so that we can get to God, but so that God can get to us. Jesus' suffering—not ours—is what heals our pain and gathers our fragments into a single whole. I believe the kingdom of God is more like a mansion with many rooms than a ladder with many rungs. We are always trying to do something. But in the end, nothing we could ever do will save us. On Judgment Day there will be no checklist or proud hero-saint. We will be so overshadowed by Christ that only Christ will remain.

o o o

It's summer as I write this, and this morning I had pancakes for breakfast. I love pancakes on July mornings. I listened to Delta blues and bluegrass—John Lee Hooker, Lester Flatt and Earl Scruggs, Robert Johnson—and made pancakes and bacon. I don't much care for the new popular recipes—pancakes with whole-wheat flour and flaxseed meal, pancakes high in fiber and calcium. I like plain, easy-to-make pancakes: Bisquick, eggs, and milk pancakes. Pancakes like the kind my mom used to make when my brother and sister and I were children. We would wake up to pancakes and Christian radio and real maple syrup and Mom and Dad talking and all the sounds and smells of six o'clock in the morning. The whole place was warm with trust and love. It was a good feeling. We knew we would never run out of pancakes. We knew we were loved.

Pancakes make me think of human nature, and about good and evil.

Lately I hear a lot of my Christian acquaintances belabor the idea that human beings are ruined and hopeless and utterly sinful. Some of them even enthusiastically tell me that "the road to hell is paved with the skulls of babies and children" (quoting Jonathan Edwards), meaning that babies who die at birth are condemned to damnation because they haven't had a chance to claim Jesus as their savior. I think these Christians really believe that the power of the cross of Jesus would be threatened if God didn't work that way. But for me, something about God glorying in burning babies makes my stomach turn. The Jesus in the Gospels just doesn't communicate anything at all like that idea of justice. I cannot see the same Jesus who said, "Let the little children come to me,"[4] also throwing them into hell forever. It is true that we all have sinned, are sinful, and are completely lost on our own and in need of a savior. The apostle Paul says this clearly. But I don't think God thinks of us as gross sea serpents. I think God loves us, carries our hearts in his heart; that he wants to gather us in his arms and give us shelter.

I think that if someone lives out a sinful nature, it is that person's insistence on ransacking the world for the diamond he already has; and if she is indeed fallen, her fall was when she first doubted that God wanted the best for her.

Adam walked with God.

In the beginning he lived in relationship with his Creator.

And in the same way a dad safeguards the innocence of his children, God had set up certain boundaries to protect our happiness, the kind of happiness children often know. When I was a child, my siblings and I didn't wake up on Saturday mornings fearing there wouldn't be pancakes for breakfast. We trusted without question that Mom and Dad would provide. To eat the forbidden fruit is in essence to say that God's provisions are insufficient, to fear that there won't be pancakes for breakfast, that God will not be what he has been from the beginning: a God of love. Like rebellious adolescents, we go to great lengths to forge our own way.

My life, at least, tells this story.

My life is full of scars, self-inflicted sins I have committed, memories I can't forget, brand marks on my body. I don't know why I keep doing things I know are bad for me, things that deep down I don't want to do. I don't know why I smoke cigarettes and play around with sex and burn myself and always try to take matters into my own hands, as if I could redefine what's right and wrong.

If only I were Joseph. Whether gross or subtle, every man has his Potiphar's Wife. Some days I'm still afraid to look myself head-on in the mirror (am I a man or a mouse?). But then, what was I thinking? God does the great work. The best I can do is put myself in a place for him to work on me, to heal me. I have tried to let holiness happen naturally, without holding up my share of the labor, but it doesn't. God waits for me to want it, and badly. Then, after I come crawling on my knees, he begins to work. And though I flounder at every turn, I must daily, hourly, home in on Christ. I must become like soft clay in his hands.

Sin is sneaky. First it will ensnare you and deprive you and then carry you away. I realized this when I read, "The evil deeds of a wicked man ensnare him; the cords of his sin hold him fast. He will die for lack of discipline, led astray by his own great folly";[5] and "Your wrongdoings have kept these away; your sins have deprived you of good."[6] You become a slave to sin. Jesus once said, "I tell you the truth, everyone who sins is a slave to sin."[7] And it ends up in death: "Godly sorrow brings repentance that leads to salvation and leaves no regret, but worldly sorrow brings death."[8]

I am amazed by the story of the criminal hanging on the cross beside Christ. "Our punishment is just," he says. "We deserve our punishment, but this man never did anything wrong in his life."[9] Jesus, speaking from a love indifferent to human merit, says to him: "Today you will be with me in Paradise."[10] This blows me away. The criminal, like me, had done nothing—could never do anything—to deserve God's generous love. Yet Christ reached out to him.

Neither righteousness nor merit can stake a claim on God's love.

It is completely unwarranted.

And what's all the more beautiful is that, although we could never hope to get to God, God can get to us, like a housebreaker, a prowler just outside the door. He's after us, jealous of our hearts. And every time I see the stripe on my shoulder or the brand on my arm I thank God for the cross of Jesus. (And on my better days, I'm audacious enough to glory in it.)

> Repent, then, and turn to God,
> so that your sins may be wiped out,
> that times of refreshing may come from the Lord.[11]

6

Yoga Truth

Enough words have been exchanged;
now at last let me see some deeds!

—GOETHE

the coffeepot poster

When reading a draft of this chapter, Stephen the Philistine circled the title and penned in the margins, in bold red ink, "What do you know about either Truth or Yoga?"!

This is exactly the kind of book that would exasperate Stephen. For in regard to truth, he would like a delineation of a doctrine, while I would rather paint pictures of my point of view. This book is a complete self-indulgence for me. Writing in the first person is a complete self-indulgence. I do not bother to defend or define. Instead, I scribble and delight. I like to try to convince Stephen of the faith by saying things like, "Christianity is an old-growth forest of the soul," rather than to articulate an apology. Stephen knows this. He also knows that I'm all talk when it comes to yoga.

I'm the kind of person who regularly thinks, *Hey, I should start doing yoga.* A few days later I'll think again, *I really should start doing some yoga.* Then, a few weeks later, *Man, I bet I'd be really great at yoga.* This thought-cycle will flop in floppy rotation for months: all the while, I sit at home—drinking too much coffee, eating inordinate amounts of pie, writing about how I should really start doing some yoga. I have thusly learned what I call the Yoga Truth:

Nothing changes if nothing changes.

I know only one yoga position: the Tadasana. For me it's the easiest one in the book. You start out by just standing there, feet together, hands at your sides for thirty seconds to a minute. It's the starting position for all other standing positions. But I have never learned where to go from there. I'm always just beginning, always at step one.

The same goes for my prayer life. I'm the kind of person who thinks about praying, collects books about prayer, but rarely prays. Whenever I start thinking, *Hey, I should start praying,* I'll read a book about prayer instead. A few days later I'll think, *I really should start praying,* and then I'll talk to my friends about how I need to start praying. Then, weeks later: *Man, I bet if I had started praying back then I would be really great at praying now.*

I also collect Bibles. Whenever I think I should start reading the Bible, I always find something wrong with every Bible on my shelf: this one has columns; that one is a paraphrase; the other one doesn't look cool. I buy about three Bibles a year. But for all the Bibles on my shelf, I rarely get down to the real business of reading the Bible.

Celibacy was a discipline to help me cultivate a Christ-centered life. A Christ-centered life is grounded in prayer and Bible reading—just to get things going, just to even start. Prayer and Bible reading are like the Tadasana position. They are necessary just to begin growing and changing into the person Christ has made you to be in him. Yet, even though I went a whole year without a single date, I still managed to avoid developing a lifestyle of prayer and Bible reading. And it's because I just never started. I was always reading and planning, getting ready to start. It's the Yoga Truth. Nothing changes if nothing changes. If you don't start what you aim to start, you'll never even, well, start.

○   ○   ○

John Chrysostom once wrote: "Prayer and praying make men temples of God." When I started my year of celibacy, I intended to spend all the energy and time I usually spent on girls on pursuing God. I wanted to become a place where God could belong, where he wouldn't be a stranger. I wanted to become a temple of God where he would be celebrated—like, in some stretched way, the way coffee shops are temples of coffee.

Everything about a coffee shop—the rich aroma, the warm lighting, the espresso bar, and the tables—is a celebration of hot, black coffee. To enter a coffee shop is to enter an experience that makes it nearly impossible not to appreciate the sacred bean. You want to get a cup of obsidian goodness. You want to go back up for a refill. And then another.

That kind of experience is what I want for God and me. I want my heart to be for Jesus what a coffee shop is for coffee. I want to be the kind of person where everything about me, everything I enjoy and serve out, is a celebration of God. Where, every day, I cannot help but grow in appreciation for the lovingkindness of Jesus Christ. I want to want God, and in venti amounts. I want to want to come back for refill after refill. Or, to turn it around, I want to serve Christ to the tired, angry, and grace-thirsty people passing by. I want to be a place where people want to come back again and again, for refill after refill—not of me, but of Christ. This metaphor is admittedly kitschy, but it's the way I think of it. I want God in this way.

And prayer that does not stop is how this can happen. Prayer makes coffee shops of our souls, places that celebrate and savor the presence and lordship of God in our lives. It must be unceasing and constant. It must become who we are.

philokalia

Well, when I was too busy reading about prayer to actually pray, I read a book called, without garnish, *The Philokalia*. It is a collection of texts on prayer and "ascesis," austere self-discipline, compiled by devout Christian monks who wrestled with *philokalia*, "love of the beautiful, the source," and unceasing prayer. These monks took sanctification seriously. They were hesychasts, men who strove to "keep stillness" in eremitic prayer. Many of them would incessantly repeat the Jesus Prayer: "Lord Jesus Christ, have mercy on me, a sinner."

The Jesus Prayer is based on Luke 18:13. A tax collector beat his chest and prayed, "God, be merciful to me, a sinner!" But this prayer is no self-recrimination. To pray the Jesus Prayer is not to go on harping on your same old struggles. I am reminded of a story told by the second-century shepherd of Hermas recounting what an old woman had said to him: "Stop dwelling on your sins and pray for righteousness!" After falling and stumbling in sin, we do not have to resign ourselves to despondency. The love of God is startling, extravagant. He heaps tenderness and favors upon us. "Here is a saying that you can rely on and nobody should doubt: that Christ Jesus came into the world to save sinners."[1] The Jesus Prayer is a rejoicing, a pleading, a surrendering to God. It is to trust in the promise of the Cross.

"Lord Jesus Christ, have mercy on me, a sinner." You pray it over and over, relentlessly, even when you don't feel like it, until the prayer becomes self-active, synchronized with your heartbeat; until it gets into your bones and takes on a life of its own. *Philokalia* is a way of spiritual transformation, a part of daily life. Gratitude arises from the lived prayer, and acceptance of all of life, a life permeated with the undeserved and unearned gift from the Father. The Jesus Prayer is an embodied celebration of the gift of salvation.

"The prayer that does not stop . . . is the Jesus Prayer: 'the uninterrupted calling upon the name of Jesus with the lips, in the spirit, and in the heart, while forming a picture of his presence and imploring his grace during every occupation—at all times, in all places, even during sleep."[2] The book of Colossians says: "Devote yourselves to prayer, being watchful and thankful."[3] The idea is that the Jesus Prayer becomes a principle for all of life. It allows us to breathe more freely, to dance more joyfully, and to sing more gratefully about the abounding love of God.

It is of little wonder that the fundamental expression of unceasing prayer is what the hesychasts called breath prayer. You breathe the prayer until it moves from the mind into the heart and finally throughout the whole body. The word of God begins to dwell richly within you, voicing itself of its own accord. "You get to see God," says Franny in Salinger's Franny and Zooey. "Something happens in some absolutely nonphysical part of the heart."[4]

Here our interest is not so much the traditional prayer directly, but applying the principle of unceasing prayer and *philokalia*—love of the beautiful, the source of truth—to daily life. The recurring theme of *The Philokalia* is striving for holistic purity; to live daily in repentance, to turn daily away from sin and toward the Christ of God.

Pray incessantly.

Prayer, at its best, is a way of life, a posture.

I discovered *philokalia* during my vow-time, but the way of *philokalia* is not only for monks and hermits, or waxing mystics like me who take unusual vows. It's also for common, working men and women, husbands and wives. Taken out of the caves of the desert fathers and mothers and the monasteries of the great orders, *philokalia* looks like, at least on the surface, ordinary life: Sundays and parties, vacations and late nights at the office, lovemaking and yard work. Without question, silence and solitude are indispensable to deep, spread-out prayer of the heart. (I will address this topic later in the book.) The Christian life begins with the inner life. These sacred monks also understood that attentiveness or watchfulness is the kernel of prayer, that to pray is to listen. "Look to the LORD and his strength; seek his face always."[5]

Philokalia in practice is life-recapturing. It awakens our God-given desire to search for the fullest life possible in relationship with him. Our battle cry should be to strive to make all of life an unceasing prayer, to get Christ into our sinews and bones, our teeth, our eyes. Because we are pilgrims on the Godward path doesn't mean we can overlook how we spend our time and how we treat our things here and now.

Daily life can become lived prayer. But the danger is to confuse daily life with prayer, which can result in prayer being replaced by, or lost in, daily life. Real prayer begins with traditional prayer—with kneeling in the quiet of the morning before God. This kind of prayer has many expressions: meditative prayer, contemplative prayer, sacramental prayer, petitionary prayer, examen, and even *lectio divina*, or "divine reading"—to name a few. But these are not the same as *philokalia*, although you cannot have one without the other. No matter how religious, the tasks of daily life are no substitute for these kinds of deliberate and spaced prayers. But if we develop a habit of quiet and intentional prayer, we inevitably carry it with us into all of life. It becomes as natural as breathing. I'm no prayer specialist, but I trust those who have gone before me.

Philokalia. It is to love the beautiful, the exalted, the source of life and truth. Love God with everything you've got. Love your roommate, your neighbor, strangers. Pray without stopping. When Christ said, "Be perfect,"[6] he meant it: "He never talked vague, idealistic gas," says C. S. Lewis.[7] Likewise, Paul exhorts the Thessalonians to "pray without ceasing."[8] And he would not have urged us to do so were it not possible.

"Pray without ceasing," says Paul (and, it should be added, he says immediately after, "give thanks in all circumstances, for this is God's will for you in Christ Jesus").[9] We often mistake this seemingly unachievable task to mean "speak" without ceasing—but only because we mistake prayer to be a monologue. It is not. Most prayer is not saying anything it all. To pray is to enter the presence of God and to listen. And to listen is a posture, a posture all of life can take on. Don't be a chatterbox, or "keep on babbling like pagans, for they think they will be heard because of their many words."[10] Because prayer is a conversation, and because God is God and we are not, a conversation with him entails at least half talk and half listening; to wit, a conversation with God would take a lifetime of listening, a lifetime of learning how to hear his voice. In his song of joy Jesus thanks the Father "for hiding these things from the learned and the clever and revealing them to little children."[11] To "pray without ceasing" is to bend low, until you are no taller than a child, and to listen to the story Christ is telling here and now and all around you.

As I've said before, I believe God sings everywhere, at all times. To pray without ceasing is to put on a posture of attentiveness, to be listening always. "Watchfulness and the Jesus Prayer," says Hesychios the Priest, "mutually reinforce one another; for close attentiveness goes with constant prayer, while prayer goes with close watchfulness and attentiveness of intellect."[12] This is the secret of spiritual transformation. The kingdom of heaven is upon you.[13] And when our hearts are inwardly disseminated by such things as business, television, preoccupation, or shallow reading, we are rendered unable to be attentive to the gift of God's present love that floods us each day.

The apostle Paul enjoins the Romans, "Rejoice in your hope, be patient in tribulation, be constant in prayer."[14] To the Colossians he wrote, "Continue steadfastly in prayer, being watchful in it with thanksgiving."[15] The Psalms are peppered with thanksgiving poetry (21; 28; 30; 65; 116; 138). Thanksgiving begins with attention. Seek

God to show you his will and truth for your life in that very moment, always. Such a sobriety and seriousness is a common motif of the book *Philokalia*. The old hesychast prayers grew into a silence, like the silence of an intense gaze, as when one stands before great art. The classic Christian idea of sobriety is to dig deep into one's self, to fight against the sin that creeps in, to "unearth the treasure buried in the field of your hearts," as Nicephorus the Solitary puts it, and "to receive the kingdom of heaven existing within you."

All of life can become a prayer, a way to listen to God. It's so beautiful to me that through the old idea of Christian sobriety we can hear the voice of God through a conversation with a friend, the time spent in rush-hour traffic, when we mow the lawn, or when we make love. The simple heart of the Christian life—including our sex lives—is learning to pray without ceasing. In a way, prayer is what Christian marriage and relationship is all about.

But it doesn't take a vow of celibacy or a marriage for us to start praying. I dedicated a whole year to becoming monkish, and it never worked because I never got down to the difficult task of praying. It's the Yoga Truth. Nothing happens if nothing happens. Start praying today. "One cannot be forever learning and forever getting ready."[16]

Whether it's practicing prayer or overcoming sin, don't put too much stock in yourself. God works harder than you might think. You might try to wrestle your way out of brambles of cynicism or sloth or pride so thick you think you're tangled beyond recognition. You throw your hands up. You take a spiritual catnap. But while you sleep, God doesn't. God is always working. Even when you feel defeated, or when God seems inactive, by faith stay awake to the activity of God within you. God was making coffee, and what you thought was the silence of God's inaction was the silence of him waiting for the coffee to percolate. For days or months or even years he was laboring in loving silence.

Don't be discouraged by your failures. If you could see my whole life story—the lapses and relapses, the pie-in-the-sky morality I make up, my insatiable appetites—you would probably put this book down in haste. I am always falling down, again and again. But I am also always trusting that Jesus is ready to save. He is listening. He is waiting. And he is quick to the rescue. It is Jesus, after all, who responds to Peter's question about how often he should forgive his brother: "Not seven times, but seventy-seven times."[17] Lord Jesus Christ, have mercy on me, a sinner. *Philokalia.* Prayer is how God plants his heart inside our hearts. It's how he changes us, fashions us into something new, makes us whole. If prayer is real, why wouldn't anyone want to spend all their time praying?

7

Crazy Love

Whoever loves, if he do not propose
The right true end of love, he's one that goes
To sea for nothing but to make him sick.

—JOHN DONNE

Here the admiring her my mind did whet
To seek thee, God. . . .

—JOHN DONNE

courtly love

I have always been interested in love, especially romantic love. Growing up I was a little obsessed. I used to tear out magazine ads of couples smooching or holding hands and hang them on my bedroom wall. I wrote love poetry. I tuned the steel strings of my guitar to a high pitch and warbled confessions of love to my high school crushes. While most boys watched baseball or action movies, I watched romantic comedies and ate buttered popcorn. It's all rather cringe-worthy, really. I harbored a secret hope during my year of celibacy that I'd find a cure for the leftover chronic, hopeless romanticism of my childhood. I never found it. But I did find that behind all the foofaraw there was a desire for something good and real—and not just a desire for a girlfriend or romance. I wasn't just some young Don Quixote fighting windmills, thinking they were giants. I didn't know it was about something more, though, until I realized that today's popular ideas about romantic love are all a hoax.

We are knee-deep in love stories. Most of them aren't really love stories at all: they're just bodice rippers, tall tales of eroticism, savvy-bachelor sex stories. We've subscribed to the wrong magazines. They're ultimately backstabbing. And, sadly, they shape what we look for in love.

Newspapers and magazines, movies and pulp fiction novels alike recount some take on amour-passion, but they don't tell the whole story of love, what it's all about. For one thing, real love is not at all the sentimental or idealized kind of love our pop stories make it out to be. Despite Hollywood's scenarios and plots of dalliance, real love is much more than a summer romance or an exciting love affair. Random and irrational relationships aren't grounded in real love.

The kind of love praised in Hollywood and cheap romance novels isn't modeled after the legacy of love found in scripture. It's a by-product from men wearing silly hats. Today's popular ideas about love don't come to us out of the story of Christ (who is behind every good thing) but instead out of a tradition popularly called Courtly Love.

○ ○ ○

It's almost too predictable that it all began in southern France. Our modern concept of love originated about eight hundred years ago, in the twelfth and thirteenth centuries, and slowly spread throughout medieval Europe, permeating Western literature and culture so thoroughly that we now take the whole idea of romantic love for granted. But the idea of Courtly Love was revolutionary at first. Nothing quite like it had existed before. Nothing has been the same since. Without Courtly Love we would have no concept of romantic love. Were it not for Courtly Love, we likely wouldn't even marry for the same reasons we do today.

What happened during this time was that, with no more barbarians to ward off, French knights were left with a lot of time on their hands. They were restless and bored. So over time, knighthood took on new meaning. Rather than just fighting to capture the gold of some looming adversary, knights often fought to capture the "silver" of their ladies' love. Some knights became troubadours, the men in silly hats, who sang songs and wrote poetry about this new kind of quest and celebrating its understanding of love in a way no one had ever done before.

The whole trend is often referred to as the "feudalization" of love because it modeled the romantic relationship between a man and a woman after the relationship between a vassal and his lord in the medieval feudal system, where a peasant would swear allegiance and services to a lord in return for work and lodging. The vassal would kneel defenseless before his soon-to-be lord and declare, "Sire, I am your man," after which he would swear by a relic.[1] In the same manner, a troubadour considered himself his lady's vassal and servant, offering his entire devotion and perfect submission. The lover's lady was his lord and he was her slave. Thus, a troubadour sang of his love, lived by his love, and would die for his love—no matter how far-fetched it became. These dramas became fashionable in the courts (hence, Courtly Love), where folks had the money and the time to entertain sensationalized love affairs.

The more the troubadours waved their silly bonnets and wrote their elaborate poetry, the more the idea of Courtly Love became something like a neo-pagan cult of love. Art at this time often depicts the troubadour's lady above him, perhaps in a castle tower, pulling him higher and higher, while his whole posture adulates toward her in supplication. C. S. Lewis has gone so far as to say that Courtly Love could be a make-believe "Religion of Love."[2] Love became a god, a good in itself. The troubadours loved the concept of love. They loved the fine-spun etiquette and elaborate rules of courtship. Lovers went so far as to seek out impediments so that their love would be made more intense. They would woo married women so that consummation would be difficult. Sometimes after merely hearing of her beauty, a knight would fall in love with a lady whom he had never even seen. The process itself came to be considered ennobling, and unsatisfied desire came to be viewed as what love is all about. Thus, for the troubadour, to gain one's love would be to lose one's desire for her, and undesirable. Which is why I think Courtly Love should be called Crazy Love. It's a love conjured out of la-la land.

In the troubadour's song, Courtly Love often began with love at first sight. Then the knight would spend time alone to cultivate his reverence for the lady from a safe distance. When it was time to declare his devotion, the result was almost always a timely and virtuous rejection (which heightened the suspense). The knight would renew his vows and swear solemn oaths, or sing songs about how he could die or how he had a lovesick tummy ache or insomnia. Sometimes Crazy Love would spur the protagonist on to heroic deeds of valor. If all went well, the troubadour and his secret lover might ride off into the sunset to secretly consummate their love (although, to keep the heartstrings taut, consummation was usually not advised).

Over time, the concept of Crazy Love spread out from the courts of the upper classes. With the Romantic Movement and the rise of the novel, the wider public eventually accepted the idea as normal. Most of us to this day are sympathetic toward a pair of "star-crossed lovers" who enjoy a romance marked by obstacles, feuding families, and a "death-marked love." Lancelot fights for Guinevere; Tristan secretly loves Iseult; Romeo woos Juliet to the death; Robin Hood saves Maid

Marian. Crazy Love has made an indelible impression on the European imagination.

This change is nowhere so evident as in marriage. Marriages in feudal society often had little to do with romantic love. They were often political and practical. Fathers arranged marriages for their daughters at the age of sixteen or younger, sometimes to men twice their age. A woman was subject to her husband's authority. It's no surprise that the troubadours had such success in wooing noblemen's wives. In an era of arranged, often heartless and intolerable marriages, Crazy Love offered romance and what looked like love and led to a change in how people view marriage. Even today, a marriage without Crazy Love looks about as attractive as boarding school. Today it is nearly impossible to think of romantic love or marriage without some Crazy Love influence.

o   o   o

But for all the troubadours got wrong, I think their story illustrates three fundamental parts of being human—and how these parts are often confused.

The first is that I believe that, unlike most women, most men don't really understand their sexuality. (I'll talk more about this in the chapter "When Kings Go Out to Battle".) We end up diving into great causes, poetry, and battles to fight. But it's not just a sex thing. Knighthood is in our blood. We need something for which to live— a purpose. In the twelfth century it was thought that only through combat could a man demonstrate valor, earn a name for himself, measure his individual worth, and glean excitement. Feudal lords viewed manual labor and commerce as too inglorious for their rank. To ease the boredom of peacetime, nobles staged tournaments where knights could fight to prove their valor. They also entertained Crazy Love. What they should have done was love their wives and work. The first thing we learn from the troubadours is that men don't need just battles to fight, causes to live and even die for: they need the right battles to fight, and the right causes to live and even die for. (Again, I'll talk more about this in the chapter "When Kings Go Out to Battle.")

The second thing we learn from the troubadours is that marriage was never meant to be about only practicality. The human heart was made for love and romance, not political agreements. Bernard of Clairvaux puts it well: "Love is an affection of the soul, not a contract: it cannot rise from a mere agreement, nor is it so to be gained. It is spontaneous in its origin and impulse; and true love is its own satisfaction."[3] Romantic love and marriage go hand in hand. Historians and anthropologists generally agree that with few exceptions conjugal love—the kind of love that typifies romantic love—has most often been a natural component of married life. Ancient Roman and medieval canonical literature and charters articulate beautifully the *affectus maritalis*, the movement of heart and commitment of the whole person that comes with *devotio*.[4] Ancient Hebrew texts, such as the story of Jacob and Rachel or the Song of Solomon, artfully illustrate romantic love. The times and places where love is believed to be incompatible with marriage are in the minority. But this doesn't mean marriage is meant to be about only romantic love. We learn from the troubadours that marriage isn't about only practicality or only romantic love. Marriage needs to be about something more. (I talk about this in the chapter "A Galactic Pizza Person.")

The third thing we learn from the troubadours is that the human heart is romantic. We love good stories, adventure, and genuine relationships. The problem with Crazy Love is that it turned romance into an end in itself. But for the Christian, romance is about more than a secret midnight rendezvous, head-over-heels flings, or savvy-bachelor sex. It's about how the light moves at a different angle. (I explore this more in the chapter "Buddha and a Pragmatic Catamaran.")

○ ○ ○

It's no coincidence that Hollywood successfully markets Crazy-Love stories to adolescents. Much like the upper classes of medieval France, when I was a teenager I had the money and the free time to entertain grand dreams of Crazy Love. I gobbled it all up. I wanted something throbbing and head-over-heels. But our ideas of romantic love are as exaggerated as our ideas of the teenager, that dramatized and glamorized youth caught in a whirlwind of sexually charged anxiety and anger, justifying any rebellion or dissipation. I can imagine that the years immediately following puberty have always been difficult and full of change, but the idea of the "teenager" is more romanticized than real, something conditioned and marketed to young adults who have the time and leisure to develop outlandish emotions and habits of mind rather than an inherent and genuine process of growing up.

There were no "teenagers" fitting this definition on nineteenth-century American farms or in medieval villages, or in ancient Rome or Israel. In the same way, when we trace romantic love back, we find it is not as old as conjugal love, sexual love, affection, or just plain lust, but the result of an idealistic kind of love invented by men in silly hats.

Though I did not know it when I was growing up, there was something more to my daydreaming and hanging pictures of marketed love stories on my wall. The troubadours didn't invent romantic love. They only exaggerated and confused what romantic love is all about. Romance and passion are not bad things. The Bible has its share of love stories, even erotic love poetry. The Bible says "Jacob loved Rachel," and I do not doubt that Adam likewise loved Eve, and Abraham, Sarah. But that the relationship between a man and a woman is a falling into a passionate, happy relationship, with a spontaneous beginning and pointed toward an indefinite end, is just not as old as the biblical models for love. The Bible gives us a deeper, more human paradigm for human relationship.

To truly love, we need a true love story. Real relationship, the kind of relationship that broadens the lives of both partners, begins with a different story—God's story.

crazy love, an italian poet, and a french monk

If it's not an accident that almost every song on the radio is about romantic love; romantic love does indeed need to be sung. And if Christianity is right—if God himself is always singing—and if all this sexual energy and heartache and passion is more than what Crazy Love makes it out to be, then perhaps all of it is telling us something about God.

Not far from where the men in silly hats were swooning over their maidens, in Clairvaux, a French monk named Bernard applied the idea of Crazy Love to monasticism. For him, the Song of Solomon was an allegory of Christ and his church. Bernard created a whole chivalry of Christianity, where monks could learn to love and swear their fealty to God. While troubadours devoted themselves to a lady, monks became troubadours devoted to the Lord. They brought chivalry into their prayer lives and interpretation of the scriptures.

Although the idea wasn't new (the Song of Solomon had long been interpreted as an allegory of God's love for the people of Israel in Jewish tradition, and of Christ's love for the church in Christian tradition), the twelfth and thirteenth centuries brought a more explicit and personally applicable meaning to the romance of faith. The idea was that God is the great lover, the ultimate romancer.

Another facet of Bernard and late medieval monasticism's adaptation of Crazy Love is that they viewed Mary, the mother of Jesus, as something like the troubadour's lady. Mary was a model of virtue, virginity, and a life free of sin; and, for this reason, monks often were considered to be troubadours for Mary. Monks thus developed a Crazy Love–like devotion to Mary. I once saw a painting that pictured this explicitly, showing Bernard of Clairvaux suckling on the spiritual milk of Mary. Like a lot of Crazy Love paintings, Bernard is kneeling before his lady (who in this case happens to be the mother of God), bent in a posture of devotion. She sits above him, enthroned, feeding him. For this painter, Crazy Love was a way to understand Bernard's spiritual journey, his relationship to Mary, and even his relationship to God.

The head-over-heels influence of Crazy Love also had enormous impact on Italian literature, especially on a poet named Dante from fourteenth-century Florence. Dante knew that not all love is good love—no matter how beautiful or exciting. He wrote:

> How far the truth is hidden from the people who aver that every love is in itself a laudable thing; because perchance its matter appears always to be good; but not every seal is good although the wax be good.[5]

Crazy Love mistakenly turned romantic love into an end in itself. But romantic love promises what romantic love by itself cannot give. The problem with the monastic adaptation of Crazy Love was that it overspiritualized romantic love. It took love out of the normal context of muddy, poetic human beings loving each other and made it a feathery tool for prayer and spiritual ardor. But for Dante, romantic love was neither an end in itself nor a mystical abstraction. It was a legitimate human experience and a pathway to God. For Dante, romantic love between a man and a woman was a kind of spiritual discipline for ordinary people living ordinary lives, with the power to teach, edify, and sanctify.

Here's Dante's story. One springtime when he was nine years old, he saw a girl named Beatrice for the first time, and it was as if the sky fell on his head. Years later, when he wrote about his story, he talked about how, when he'd pass her on the street, her "Good morning!" hit him like a kick in the solar plexus. In Italian, "good morning" (salute) can mean not only "good health" and "salutation" but also "salvation." In Dante's poetry that greeting, that "Good morning!"

became a symbol for what romantic love is all about. He never tells us if Beatrice, the name he gave her (which means "the bringer of blessings"), was her real name.

For Dante, loving Beatrice was like asceticism or monasticism or evangelism, or any other spiritual discipline. He never married Beatrice. He never even dated her. Indeed, we can hardly say he even fell in love with her—at least in the popular connotations of the phrase. With Beatrice, Dante's experience was more like awe or wonder. Love for Dante was a state of heightened consciousness.

Dante put to verse what thousands have stammered in tattered phrases: the common, ordinary and astonishing experience of discovering that someone exists. You have probably experienced something like it—that moment a particular someone walked into the room. It was as if you had been color-blind and, in one fell swoop, you were given the whole spectrum of color.[6]

For many of us the memory of this innocent beholding, of simply being inspired and charged by the very sight of a beautiful person, is lost in the barrage of locker rooms and Playboys.

But it happens.

Men and women are discovering one another every day.

For Dante, the beauty of Beatrice was a reprimand and a summons: a reprimand because her beauty convicted him of the sin in his life, a summons because her beauty inspired him to pursue holiness. Botticelli's drawings of Dante and Beatrice are similar to the Crazy Love paintings in that Beatrice is above Dante, and he is beneath her, as if in prayer. But Beatrice is to these pictures what a needle is to a compass. She points the way. As Dante's gaze reaches out for her, she directs his gaze to God. She is a finger pointing Godward. Dante looks to her and she directs his gaze to the stars.

For Dante, romantic love is a way God reaches out to find us and bring us to him. The image of God in you loves the image of God in your sweetheart. She is a better image of God than the Grand Canyon, or the whole night sky. She is a carriage of grace, a God-bearer. She is a road sign indicating the road that leads to God.

The beatrician way is a way of kingdom living. Beatrice sanctified Dante, encouraged him on his spiritual journey. In a way, she herself didn't do anything. We often pray that God would work through us, that he would use us as instruments of his grace. When we get the opportunity to share our faith with an unbelieving friend and he or she comes to accept Christ as his or her God and Savior, we would never say that we did the great work. God did the work. We were a part of it. We participated. But Christ was in it and behind it all the time. In the same way, Beatrice was a minister of grace to Dante.

The difference between a troubadour's love stories and Dante's love story couldn't be more stark. Neither of them loved the actual woman. But Crazy Love was in love with love. The adventures and comforts of love were ends in themselves. Against this background, as Bernard and Dante knew, little for the Christian is an end in itself, even romantic love. Nothing is wrong with writing love poetry or singing love songs. But why we love and what we communicate to others through love can be wrong.

Together, Dante and Bernard of Clairvaux give us a good start at looking at love without all the baggage and furbelow of Crazy Love. Romantic love might not be how we can reach God. But romantic love can put us in a place for God to reach us. A Godward love. It's a love so good it will make you fall off your bicycle.

8

A Galactic Pizza Person

Happy those, three or more times over
United by an unbroken bond
Whose love, unmarred by bitter strife
Will not release them till their dying day.

—HORACE

bob's java hut

In springtime, Minneapolis wakes up. We come out from our caves and our clapboard-siding houses, hair messy, yawning, eager to breathe fresh air again. We vacuum our floors, straighten our cupboards, and open our windows to listen to the songbirds. But in the summertime, we grill steaks on our backyard patios or go down to the lakes. The lakes are the city's watering holes, the places to meet girls and rollerblade and play volleyball, to stop for drinks at the Tin Fish and watch the sailboats.

Summer is also the time for hot coffee. And so I am sitting with Karen, my friend from church, at Bob's Java Hut, the caffeine outpost on Lyndale where the bikers hang out. Here you can expect to rub elbows with bearded drywall hangers, wannabe punk rockers, and hard-luck java-mongers alike.

When the weather is right, the employees at Bob's lift a big garage door that opens to a sidewalk with plastic tables that get hot in the sunlight. Motorcycles line the curb. The sidewalk is where the smokers loiter. It's also where Karen and I can drink our coffee and watch traffic. I like Karen. I call her Karen the Otolaryngologist. She goes to medical school and studies diseases of the ear, nose, and throat. She talks about science and math a lot and I like to get lost in her words, words like: bisector, rheumatological, and gradient. It's almost too bad that our conversations tend to revolve around Christian spirituality, because in consequence, I don't get to hear her talk science and math. It's okay, though: Christianity has its own full-bodied, almost ritzy words, words like omnipotent, degeneracy, triune, and apocalyptic.

Karen and I talk about Jesus a lot because we're both going through a lot of transition. I think we're like many other Christians our age. Those of us who grew up in the church eventually reach a point in life where we need to make our faith in Jesus our own. We try to imagine how Christianity's going to mold our adult lives, and then we try to act on it.

Today, however, we've been taking our coffee over small talk and long silences. I can tell that she has something on her mind. She sighs and looks out at the street. I love the people here at Bob's. I love watching the tattooed vegans talk. I love listening to the lesbians with shaved heads laugh while the old men read newspapers.

"Tyler, I don't mean to hit you with a ton of bricks or anything," she begins and I pause, listening, "but I'm seriously feeling like my Christianity is too abstract and removed, too distant from my actual life." She sips her coffee; then holds it up, gesturing, as she speaks.

"It's like, here are Jesus and Peter and Paul, and they lived these radical lifestyles; and there are people around the world today who are killed for their faith. But if things keep going the way they're going with my boyfriend, I'll probably just end up being a science-geek soccer mom. Have a house. Maybe a part-time job. Maybe even cook. You know, something . . . boring."

I nod, not really knowing what to say. Not a ton of bricks, but she was serious.

"Boring compared to Jesus and those guys in the Bible, or just boring in general?" I ask.

"Both, I think. I just feel like there is a dissonance between that life and the 'kingdom life' you see in the gospel. *That* life is so extreme, so out there." She held her cup in both hands and looked over it before taking a sip. "If our lives are supposed to emulate Christ's, how can we justify having a house with a picket fence, a family, a couple of cars in the garage? Christianity just doesn't seem domestic. Sometimes I feel like I shouldn't be here but over someplace like India, living dangerously for Christ."

I agree, sort of, I guess; but not really. And I'm surprised to find that the more I think about it, the more angry I get. It might be because I feel that marriage has gotten a bad rap these days. So few of my friends talk about it positively. The word is practically taboo in conversation. Or maybe it's because I've got spiritual hang-ups. Maybe the only reason I can't relate to what Karen is saying is because sometimes it feels as if all I want to do is get married. I feel real bad about it, as if I should want to go on mission trips or move to Indonesia to preach the gospel. But all I want to do is stay home. I want to be Father Tim. I don't want to learn other languages or first aid or smuggle Bibles into other countries. I don't even like to read the international news. I think this might be a serious flaw in my personality.

"Karen," I say after a time, "did you know I've had this secret fear that I'm going to turn out to be just like Jonah?" Somebody kicks his bike to a purr and I pause, examining the shadows that splash across our table. She sets down her glass cup. I continue, "I've got this complex. I think that God is out to get me—that if I really surrender my life plans to the divine plans he has for me, that he'll trick me. I'm afraid he's going to call me to Africa or Indonesia, when all I want to do is stay home."

"Don't you think that if God wanted you to go to Africa, he'd put the desire to go in your heart?" she asks.

"See, that's just it! I don't want God to change my heart, to make me want to go to places I don't want to go to or to do things I don't want to do." I swallow. And then I confess something I know I'll regret sharing. It makes me feel just plain rotten and shallow. But it's the truth, and so I tell Karen anyway. "I also have this fear that God is going to trick me into marrying a tuba."

Thankfully, she doesn't judge me but laughs. "A tuba, Ty?"

"Yeah. It's like I know it's probably superficial and lame that I want to marry a Total Babe. I'm afraid God's going to trick me, change my heart so that I fall in love with an Oompa because she has a beautiful heart; and then I'll wake up years later, shocked and confused by my situation, wondering how I ended up in Africa, or wherever, with this . . . woman." I feel awful. I do.

"Tyler," she says, smiling, "I don't think God is out to trick you. That's just not the way he works—you know that. He's not going to trick you into marrying someone you're really not attracted to, a big Oompa." She says the word childishly and smiles, as if to say, don't-be-such-a-baby.

And I do know. There's a tattoo parlor above Bob's, the Uptown Tattoo, and a bald man walks out with a bandage on his arm, trying to pretend he isn't proud or excited about his new ink, as if he does this kind of thing all the time. I watch him walk down the sidewalk like a new man, a new man with a new and beautiful blue tattoo. I remember when I got my first tattoo. I felt like a new man. But nothing changed. "Those that cross the sea," says Horace, "change their sky not their souls." But here's to trying, I guess.

"Karen, I do know that. I guess the only reason I bring it up is because I've realized that the way we tend to think about things—like the questions you were just telling me about, with marriage and missions—isn't right. It's just not right to think that mission work is something we do away from home, and that home life is, well, home life—not ministry."

Even as I'm telling her this, images materialize in my mind of the bold, vagabond life of Jesus and his apostles, and the stark discipline of medieval itinerant preachers. I think of the desert fathers and of Paul. I think of celibate nuns. I think of missionaries. Aren't their lives patent examples of an extreme life in God's service? Karen's concerned about whether her desire to be a wife and mother aligns with the radical and celibate life of Christ that's written about so beautifully in the Bible.

At first glance the kingdom life and wedded life do seem disconnected. "Get thee a wife, get thee a wife!" just doesn't ring like, "Go out into the whole world and preach the gospel to all creation, baptizing them in the name of the Father and the Son and the Holy Spirit."[1] In fact, one might wonder if a world of supper tables, sex, and wedding anniversaries is a justifiable way to imitate Christ in our lives. In the Gospels we do not see a bed and board but an open road. I can't help but wonder with Karen, shouldn't the Christian life be one more of extremes? Shouldn't we all heed Jesus' answer to the rich young ruler when he asked what he must do to be saved: "Go and sell your possessions and give to the poor, and you will have treasure in heaven; then come, follow me"?[2] Should we drop our nets, so to speak, abandon home and hearth, and "allow the dead to bury their own dead"?[3]

I demur: "But Karen, what if the real ministry, the most important ministry, doesn't begin with leaving but with staying? What if God's kingdom doesn't start far away but in our own homes, right here in Minneapolis? What if the most important thing you could do for Christ here on earth is get married?"

Karen's watching two gorgeous bikers take off their helmets, all muscles and mustaches. I don't think she thinks about bikers in quite the same way I do, as monastics. She probably doesn't think the mustaches are cool either. But I'm building a whole theory of marriage on my daydream of a motorcycle, and I feel that being around bikes helps me put words to what I'm thinking.

"The way I see it," I say, caffeinated, sitting on the edge of the plastic picnic table, "Christ is this enormous historic reality that touches every and all aspects of human life. Jesus Christ is God of all things, not just some things. And God designed us for marriage, like Adam and Eve, for a reason, a beautiful reason. And I think it's because it's a way he can show us a tiny piece of who he is."

We talked for a long time that day. I still think about what Karen said. Karen's question is important because it raises this question: What is the good of a Christian marriage?

a galactic pizza person

My friend Catherine, from the coffee shop where I work, is a screenwriter. I sometimes walk down to her apartment to smoke cigarettes and drink wine from coffee mugs and listen to Bob Dylan or Iron & Wine on her turntable. Written around the perimeter of her living room in cheap acrylic paint are the words "We are writing, we are writing, we are writing. . . ." I've always found it good to write with other writers, especially when they're so different from me. It's convicting to be friends with someone like Catherine. She cares about people and the environment and animals more than most people I know, including myself. I wish more Christians were like her.

The other night we were sitting on her stoop when a Galactic Pizza man drove by. Galactic Pizza is in Uptown Minneapolis, our stomping grounds. Their deliverymen (Catherine would have me say delivery-people) drive around in tiny electric cars dressed like superheroes, saving the neighborhood one great pizza at a time. Last year a guy on the street yoinked an old lady's purse and ran. A Galactic Pizza person making a delivery saw the robbery and chased the thief down, demanding back the purse. The thief was apparently so startled by the Superman garb that he handed the purse over readily, as if grateful to wash his hands of the matter.

So as I said, Catherine and I are sitting on her front stoop when the Galactic Pizza person goes by, and she tells me about how her friend and roommate has just moved out and how she doesn't like the silence of an empty apartment. She tells me how she listens to Elliott Smith nonstop these days because she's lonely, and about how she once got high and ordered some Galactic pizza just because she needed a knight in shining armor to break the silence, the loneliness. That night the Galactic Pizza person was her hero. Catherine's an idealist in her own way, like me, and almost apologizes for being afraid of silence, of being lonely. But I can't point any fingers. I don't think we were meant to be alone. It runs against who we are, goes against the nature of things.

Catherine says she doesn't so much miss talking with her friend, but misses just being able to be grumpy or eccentric with her, maybe order some Galactic pizza; just be, really.

I can't help but think of what God says about Adam in the Garden of Eden: "It is not good for man to be alone."[4] At first it didn't make any sense to me that Adam would be lonely. The Genesis story says that God walked in the garden. So Adam didn't have to consort with giraffes or kangaroos, but could interact with God himself. How could he be lonely in any way? It seems counterintuitive to say it, but in some way, God was not enough. He must have made it so. God was God and Adam was Adam. Adam was inferior to God and superior to the animals, but equal to no one. So Adam needed a complement, a collateral love, one of his own kind.

Sometimes I can relate to Adam's loneliness, and I see women every day. I think the experience of loneliness is pretty much universal, a familiar pang, a need that must be met. For some of us our earliest childhood fears are of loneliness, a fear that does not abate with age. How many lonely, old men have sought Hemingway's "clean, well-lighted space"? "One cannot live this solitary life," wrote Darwin, "with groggy old age, friendless and cold, and childless staring one in one's face, already beginning to wrinkle."[5] To be ignored, forgotten, or isolated are biting winds against which we build the strongest buffers. We need more than mud, more than food and water and hot showers. We need poetry. We need relationship, community.

"It's not good for man to be alone!" And I can just see God rolling up his sleeves, like an artist, to make Eve—not from the dust of the earth like Adam, but from Adam's own side. "At last!" Adam tenderly gasps when he sees her for the first time. "This is now one of my own, bone of my bones and flesh of my flesh."[6] She is his Galactic Pizza delivery person, sent to break the silence, his "helpmeet." I once read that the Hebrew phrase translated "helpmeet" (*ezer kenegdo*), is "a notoriously difficult word to translate,"[7] and carries far greater meaning than merely "helper." It means "lifesaver," and is used elsewhere only of God. "There is no one like the God of Jeshurun, who rides on the heavens to help you."[8] An *ezer kenegdo* is a hero, a Galactic Pizza person.

By extracting a rib from Adam, God seems to highlight Adam's incompleteness, to stamp upon his figure an indelible mark of need. And perhaps it is to remind us that it is not good for any of us to be alone.

Being in relationship with God does not in itself seem to suffice.

What if God made it so that what we need over and above merely existing is to know and love another person, and to be known and loved in return? As Kierkegaard puts it, "What I am through her she is through me, and neither of us is anything by oneself, but we are what we are in union. Through her I am Man."[9]

Here is something wonderful to reflect on, even though I do not understand it. Augustine says that a good picture of God is seen not in only Adam or in only Eve but in both, together; that husband and wife side by side make a picture of God. Paul says something to this effect, as we've read before: "Husbands, love your wives. There is a great truth hidden here and this mystery is vast—it is the very symbol of Christ and the church."[10]

○ ○ ○

By "marriage" most of us mean the formal union of man and woman, recognized by law, and intended to last a lifetime. But I think what makes a marriage Christian is something much more poetic and severe. In the Genesis story, the exchange of a vow, or social convention, or sexual union, or cohabitation do not in themselves make a marriage. Rather, the Bible states that husband and wife are to be one flesh.[11] I think this oneness refers to much more than just sex. I think in Adam and Eve there is a real correspondence. Each was the other's second half, the fulfillment of the other's image-bearing, their reflecting of God. Offering community and relationship, Eve is to Adam another self.

I feel that the way our culture prizes the individual turns one of the best ideas for good living upside down. We have turned the good neediness of mud on its head. So many people today think marriage "threatens" the individual or that sex "risks" children. If we could just see things right side up, we'd see that a good marriage protects the individual and sex offers the potential of children. Christian marriage works as the basis for bringing meaning, belonging, and obligation to daily life.

The upside-down idea of savvy-bachelor autonomy screams "I," but Christian marriage, like Christian celibacy, sings "We"—a whole and holy oneness. And for all we know, this oneness is the foundation, the very marrow, of the church, for it is the setting of the daily, real, and troublesome world. And this is precisely why it has so much potential for good.

We tend to interpret the image of "Christ the Bridegroom" as a metaphor for understanding Christ. But it is not. We cannot assume that divine things are revealed to us by means of human categories, as if the human were real and the divine were not. It is the other way around. All things human derive from God's reality. And I don't think God uses human images to describe heavenly things just to help us understand what we would otherwise not be able to understand. It is we who are made in his image, not he in ours. As I said before, calling God "Father" is not a figure of speech; he is Father, and all human fathers are but shadows or echoes of the real thing. In the same way, I believe human marriage is not definitive of divine reality but draws its meaning from the relationship between Yahweh and Israel, from the final union of Christ and his church, and from the Trinity. God's is the archetype; ours is the ectype. "God is love,"[12] says John; and, interestingly enough, the Genesis story narrates: "In the image of God he created them; male and female he created them."[13]

Catherine's night of getting high and ordering pizza is just a limited picture of the way human beings are. Made in the image of God, like a snapshot into his heart, humans naturally desire love and community. Echoing the interrelational mystery of the Trinity, we need others physically, emotionally, intellectually, and spiritually. To be utterly alone is to be, in some way, incomplete.

building blocks

To be born again is to be tied to God. And when we are tied to God, we are tied to one another. The love that grows out of your salvation is never just between you and God. It always grows deeper and wider, spreads out. The love of Christ inevitably builds community.

Love and community are at the heart of what it means to be human. To remove either would be to remove the lungs or the liver: the patient wouldn't survive. For the most part, humans have to live together in community. The hermits, the Robinson Crusoes, are the exception, not the norm. People love to be around people. There is a joy inherent in community, a natural sweetness it brings to life. And I believe marriage and family are at the heart of any earnest and reward-ing human life—if not for everyone, at least for the vast majority.

Aristotle, in his work the Politics, says that by nature humankind is a "political animal," a communal, social being. I think that Aristo-tle is right. Paul says it better in his letter to the Romans: "We, who are many, are one body in Christ, and individually we are members one of another."[14] By "members" I don't think he meant something like a member of Congress or a member of a bowling league (that is, interchangeable units of a collective). Rather, Paul meant some-thing more organic, like a family or organs of the human body. The organs of a body aren't interchangeable. They are different from, and complementary to, one another. Each serves a different function that equally makes up the whole. I believe that to be baptized is not only to mingle with God in some mysterious way, but also to get tangled up in and adopted into the whole company of saints. The "in-Godding" of man, as Charles Williams has called it, is also the "in-othering" of humans. The union of humans with humans and humans with God is knotted together.[15]

Sadly, Enlightenment individualism, some uses of technology, some feminist ideologies, and some of the ideas behind the sexual rev-olution have made us increasingly autonomous and disconnected. I think individualism has so shaped our attitudes and actions that even Christian living has been made into something solitary. But Christian-ity opposes individualism from its every pore. Christ affirms not only our need for others, but also our need for community; he demands it of us. It is part of building the City of God, of becoming the body. Christ is not only in our quiet times or prayer closets. Our Lord is in the least of these.[16] And I think the second great commandment is how you obey the first: you cannot love the Lord your God with all your heart if you do not love your neighbor as yourself.[17] Even ascet-ics are communal; even monks are brotherly; and every layperson is summoned in some degree to be congregational; that is, to participate in a church community.

I think that, in the same way, at least socially speaking, marriage is prior to the household; as the household is prior to the city, so too is marriage prior to the congregation, just as the congregation is prior to the universal church. The healthiest congregations are not those made up primarily of singles, but those filled with families, with parents and their children; where pastors preach to the sounds of sniffles and crayon scribbles and crying babies; where husbands and wives and celibates worship side by side, a living picture of Christ and his church right in front of your eyes.

Kingdom life and wedded life are bound up in each other. What if the steady, undercurrent work of God isn't so much accomplished through our Walmart-sized churches and international projects, but through the day-to-day self-surrendering between one man and one woman loving each other, being committed to each other in marriage, and the overflow of that love to their children? For isn't marriage a mix of mutual admiration and esteem, sex, kisses, communication and care, and at times admonishment and correction? I wonder if in sharing common projects and in protecting and caring about the personal growth of the beloved, Christian marriage can become a partnership of high risk and adventure in the activity of God?

If such an approach to marriage strikes you as strange, it's probably because Crazy Love thinking has become so pervasive as to be invisible. We forget that, historically, men and women have married for a great many reasons other than a passionate, romantic love. Marriage is also about community, about family and spirituality, about our relationships to the world, and about expressing our identities as human beings. The belief that marriage should be foremost about Crazy Love is a relatively new and, I think, destructive idea—destructive not just for the pleasure of marriage but also for our spiritual lives. Marriage is a spiritual discipline.

○ ○ ○

In a Christian marriage something is being communicated, prepared, and built up, something that helps us better understand God's heart.

My friend Karen the Otolaryngologist is right to wonder if Christian marriage is as important as mission work. But I think we need to remember that God uses ordinary people and events to do extraordinary things. He doesn't necessarily want our warehouse churches and our time lines to Armageddon or our multimedia technologies. I believe he's waiting, as a child waits for the recess bell in class, for us to discover that he is actually in our own neighborhoods, our own friendships and marriages, and that he wants to make something beautiful.

Ordinary Time, the time from Pentecost to the day before Advent, is a time for growth in Christ, a time to redeem ordinary life. I wonder if God is using our everyday humanness, our mud and poetry—our aging bodies, our fickle emotions, our wandering minds, our art—to build his kingdom. In some sense, marriage is like enrolling in Christianity 101. If what the apostle Paul says is true, Christian marriage, along with celibacy, is one of the most at-hand pictures of God and eternity we have. Who would want to miss anything?

○ ○ ○

In marriage we seek oneness. Yet for as close as the marriage knot ties two people, it does not make them homogeneous. I don't think the Bible's idea of "one flesh" means identical or indistinguishable; but rather, correlative, complementary, even opposite. Eve is wholly separate and unique, a complete and individual personality apart from Adam. He is Man (Hebrew, *ish*), and she is Woman (Hebrew, *isha*). God's design for love is almost a contraction. Two are to be one. They are similar, but not at all the same. It is with great wisdom that Kahlil Gibran says in *The Prophet*:

But let there be spaces in your togetherness.
And let the winds of the heavens dance between you.[18]

I think the biggest mistake you can make in marriage is to assume you know everything about your spouse. I imagine that for some, sadly, it's not until their beloved is gone that they realize how much they didn't know them at all, that their assumed familiarity left the other feeling isolated and misunderstood.

It's important to remember that to be one flesh is not to be identical. Years ago I read a portrait of married life that has stuck with me. Apparently for a Sioux warrior the duty of prayer comes before any other duty. He rises at dawn and walks down to the water's edge and dives in (or throws handfuls of water into his face). Afterward he stands to face the dawn and offer up his unspoken prayers. His wife's devotions may precede or follow his, but she may never accompany him. "Each soul must meet the morning sun, the new sweet earth, and the Great Silence alone!"[19] I read this description at the same time I was reading, over and over again, *Letters to a Young Poet* by Rainer Rilke: "I hold this to be the highest task of a bond between two people," says Rilke, "that each should stand guard over the solitude of the other. . . . It is a question in marriage, to my feeling, not of creating a quick community of spirit by tearing down and destroying all boundaries, but rather a good marriage is that in which each appoints the other guardian of his solitude."[20]

For Rilke, the great question of marriage is whether you are willing not only to stand guard over the personality, the individuality, of the beloved, but also to let this person stand at the gate of your own personality. When it comes to loving others as an-other, another self, we are inclined to flee such differences. We often seek out someone who is more like us. But if we can overcome this impulse, we may enter relationships that can help us reach beyond, far beyond, ourselves.

Catherine from the coffee shop helped me understand the idea of otherness this way. She says screenwriting is different from writing fiction. Unlike in a novel, with screenwriting you can't write what the characters think; you can write only about what the characters do or say. You can't get directly into their heads and hearts. It's almost like real life. No matter how close you get to your spouse, you can't get inside of him or her: no matter how much you care or how badly you want to, he or she will always be independent from you, thinking thoughts you can't experience, experiencing feelings that you will never be able to fully feel. To me this is a difficult thing about the Christian idea of marriage as one flesh: no matter how much you try to become one, you can never know someone completely.

Marriage is one of the best ideas on earth. The beautiful thing about it is that what Adam lacks, God makes available in Eve. Where Adam is stuck in the old way, she points out the improvement of the new. What he cannot see, she just sees. And it goes the other way around. Being different is a good thing. And so I sometimes wonder if despite how important it is to be locked together, to be allies, one flesh, maybe the desire to become so fully one that there is no distinguishable difference between you and your spouse isn't the point. Maybe we shouldn't necessarily try to know everything. Maybe we are just supposed to have our beloved close to us, breathing; just have her around, just being free to be grumpy or eccentric with her, just being. Maybe we were just meant to belong together, two widely different people bound up and tangled like a knot that can't be untied.

Catherine used to have a promise ring engraved with "I am my beloved's and my beloved is mine,"[21] but she lost it in Austria. She doesn't miss it anyway, she confesses, while carefully lifting a Donovan album from the turntable. She starts looking for Radiohead's Kid A. She had already changed her mind a long time ago about sex and chastity. But still, the phrase keeps running through my mind, like a melody. I am my beloved's and my beloved is mine. Catherine thinks she lost Radiohead, and the phrase fills my mind in the silence: I am my beloved's and my beloved is mine. There is something of quiet and of joy in these words, something worth working toward.

○ ○ ○

It amazes me how seemingly comfortable Jesus Christ is with his guttersnipe, ragamuffin church. Church is what it has always been: grubby sinners who have been born again living out their new life in Christ together, working to build the kingdom of God-With-Us, here and now.

And, if you're not called to celibacy, marriage is the first conjunction.

Along with the celibate calling, our marriages are the building blocks of God's new rule.

Christ not only attended the wedding feast; he blessed it. Marriage is God's good gift to us. And as he turned water into wine, maybe Jesus wants also to take something as ordinary as marriage and turn it into something extraordinary. Maybe Christian marriage can become a way of the soul, a spiritual discipline.

Maybe Christian marriage can be like that place where Jacob camped on his journey toward Haran, where he had a vision of angels ascending and descending a ladder and God, standing above it, had revealed his covenant. Maybe, like Jacob, we will awake saying, "Surely the LORD is in this place—and I did not know it!"[22] And maybe we can model our marriages after Bethel, the "house of God," and revere them, saying, "How awesome is this place! This is none other than the house of God, and this is the gate of heaven."[23]

9

How to Date Like a Christian

Though this be madness, yet there is method in't.

—SHAKESPEARE

my list

It was late autumn, and I was passing the Victoria's Secret at the intersection of Lake and Hennepin when I realized that I actually do have a list of what I'm looking for in a spouse. I know I said in chapter 2 that I don't like the idea of spousal lists. I really don't. But when I passed Victoria's Secret it made me think about underwear and sex and women in general, and it made me think about what I'm looking for in a wife. And then I realized: not only do I have a list, I have a very specific list. It's just that I'm in denial about it. I don't know why Victoria's Secret triggered it all, honestly. That store makes me squirm. I wish I could be more mature about it all. Whenever I pass it I try to pretend that I don't even notice. I try extra hard to look like I'm more interested in the traffic or the sky than I am in seeing women in their underwear. The point is I was at the intersection of Lake and Hennepin when I had my Victoria's Secret revelation—when I realized what I'm looking for in a wife.

When I got home I wrote all my thoughts on the back of an envelope from that month's utilities bill. A few days later I invited my friend Karen the Otolaryngologist over for sandwiches. I told her, with some enthusiasm, about my Victoria's Secret revelation and asked her what she thought of my list.

I had it all organized in my head: four specific things I'm looking for. I told her how the first thing I thought about was how, since I tend to think so hard that I get depressed, I would like it if my wife had a natural disposition to joy. She may be loud or quiet, introverted or extroverted—it doesn't matter. I just want someone who can be emotionally independent from me, who won't swing with my stereotypical artist's moods. (It's a fault of mine—I'm moody. I squirm in the movie theater when the dramatically depressed and sporadic artist is caricatured. This is because I paint and make music and write poetry and am lost in those media to the point of sadness. I fit the artist-cliché horribly.) Anyhow, I told Karen that my future wife doesn't have to be always happy or always pleasant: that's just not being human. Everyone generally has a natural mood or aura, and I'm attracted to women with a natural disposition to joy.

Karen looked at me with a twinkle in her eye. Her only comments thus far had been "Hmm," and, "Interesting . . . ," and she always has a comment, so I could tell she probably thought the whole thing was cute or something, and I became suddenly embarrassed and then, maybe because I'm a smoker, I all of a sudden needed to do something with my hands. I got up and started making the sandwiches. She followed me into the kitchen. Autumn was in full color, and she asked me where she could hang the scarf and flannel she had worn on her way over to my apartment. Of all the seasons, I love autumn the most. The whole world is crisp and bright and peaking, and girls like Karen wear beautiful mittens and scarves and hand-knitted hats. As

I started to make the sandwiches, I grabbed turkey, salami, pepper cheese, orange marmalade, thick slices of sourdough bread, and an apple (apple, thinly sliced, makes a sandwich).

I continued to tell her about my list. As I put the bread in the toaster oven, I told her about how I would like it if my wife had a consciousness of the depths, as well as a love for the heights. Karen said she didn't understand what I was getting at and so I told her, "I want someone who is crazy in love with Jesus, someone who rejoices in God's love. But I also want someone for whom sin and depression and hard struggles are very real."

"So wait, you're saying you want your future wife to have been hurt or depressed?" Karen interjected, clearly having fun with my Victoria's Secret revelation.

"No," I said, realizing how wooden my new criteria for a wife were sounding, "I guess I just don't want her to be sheltered. I want to be able to share the whole of the human experience with her—not just its joys, but also its hardships."

And then, in a way only a bookish scientist could put it, Karen said, "You know, Ty, it seems to me that the whole concept of a wife as a concept is so colossal and nebulous that—right now, at least for you—no decisive and perspicuous analysis of its concept can be undertaken without sounding, well, procrustean." By which I took her to say, It's ironic that you've made a list since you're always preaching sermons in bars and dining rooms about how incarcerating lists can be to a human person in relationship.

Touché. I spread the mayonnaise on two slices of bread and the orange marmalade on the other two. I started to build each sandwich. Karen's right, of course. She knows it. And she knows she can completely rain on my parade. In a moment of incredible wit, I respond, "It would also be refreshing if she spoke her mind," and wink at her. After some thought, I continue: "It would be nice if she were able to put words to what she is thinking or feeling—at least most of the time. I know sometimes we're just not able to understand, let alone articulate, what we're feeling or experiencing; but still, generally speaking, I would like to be able to talk with her about pretty much anything." I put our toasted sandwiches on plates, Karen grabbed the chips from the counter, and we headed back into the living room.

"You want your wife to be thoughtful and articulate," Karen clarified.

"Yeah," I said, sitting on the couch. "I just feel like for me talking and talking a lot about a lot of things is the most important part of, well, real intimacy. I want a woman who is reflective and thoughtful, someone with an opinion and who isn't afraid to tell it like it is." I am obsessed with talking—almost as much as I am with the importance of standing guard of the personality of the beloved. J. B. Priestley combines these two ideas beautifully: "Talk demands that people should begin, as it were, at least some distance from one another, that there should be some doors still to unlock. Marriage is partly the unlocking of those doors, and it sets out on its happiest and prosperous voyages when it is launched on floods of talk."[1] Any good marriage bursts into being on volleys and spates of talk. I'm looking for a woman who is honest, vulnerable, funny in her way, and frank, and who will simply not settle for a life without greater meaning.

"Tyler, you haven't mentioned sex or good looks yet," Karen interjected between bites, and looked at me in playful accusation. "What about your fear of waking up next to a tuba?" (She said this because she knows I think I need to be fiercely sexually attracted to a woman. I want to turn up Marvin Gaye's "Let's Get It On" and pour the wine out of sheer and uncontrollable, helpless attraction. I don't need her to look like a Victoria's Secret model, but I need her to be beautiful— inside and out. Beauty like a blooming. Beauty that will flower as we get older together.)

I laughed. "Yeah, Karen, if I were honest, I would have put that one up at the top of my list. I just didn't want to come across as shallow as a savvy bachelor." I ate a chip. "But you're right: I want a wife who is all woman."

So that's what I wrote on the utilities envelope: (1) a natural disposition to joy; (2) a consciousness of the depths and the heights; (3) articulate, opinionated, and thoughtful; (4) all woman, tout court. But talking to Karen, I realized that there is more. For example, as I tend to be poetical and visionary, it would definitely also be a plus if she were able to counter my abstractions with practical wisdom. Nothing is so refreshing as a frank and horribly practical retort like, "Ty, have you prayed about this yet?" or, "Ty, stop putting this off, and please stop talking to me about it: just go out there and get it done!"

Glasses would be nice too: thick librarian glasses, with a sparkly chain. Librarian glasses just slay me.

I'm really, really bad at budgeting and math as well, so if she were number savvy, I would be all the more happy.

After we finished our sandwiches, Karen grabbed some Izze sodas from the fridge. I think she liked the list because as she sat back down with her Izze and curled her legs up on the couch she just smiled and said—like a scientist, I think—"Interesting."

o o o

An irony of me writing about what I'm looking for in a wife right now is that I've pretty much given up believing she's out there, or at least will be any time soon. Right now, I think, it would be good for me to just date some girls. Besides, even though I'm not hoping with each first date, This might be the one!, I do think dating is one of the best ways to get to know if someone is marriage material. Some Christians have a hard time dating because of the Chastity Cult (I'll talk about this in the next chapter) or because of sheer un-inspiration. But I've recently been dating all sorts of different girls, and I have learned a few simple steps about how you can date like a Christian.

step 1: find a date

I think as a general rule, if you like a girl, you should ask her out on a date.

Don't be a codfish.

Man up and take her out. Make yourself presentable and sally forth into the world.

And if you live in Minneapolis and you're hurting for ideas, I know of so many great places to go out in my neighborhood. You can drink Grain Belt beer and shoot pool at the C.C. Club, a local bar full of punk rockers, hipsters, and tattooed, lumberjack-looking people. You can walk around Lake Calhoun at sunset, when the world is that beautiful blushing color. You can dress up and go out to eat at Tum Rup Thai, drink pinot noir at the candlelit French bistro Barbette, bowl at Bryant Lake Bowl, or just gawk at the Walker Art Center. If you've got itchy feet, you can take a day trip to Duluth or to Stillwater, or cruise Highway 61. You can also just stay home and play Scrabble or chess, watch *Shrek*, listen to vinyl, or make sushi. I think there is also great merit in the picnic—like the grand old ones our grand-parents would lay out. Call up a few friends, invite your sweetheart, pack a basket of sandwiches, a Frisbee, and promenade to the nearest hilltop or park.

Dating isn't as scary or as bad as some Christians make it out to be. It's okay. Really, it is. I once studied the history of dating, which is as interesting as it is morally neutral. If you're a Christian, you are called to build God's kingdom on earth through either mar-riage or celibacy; and if, as Paul puts it, you "burn with passion,"[2] you must set about the business of finding a lifelong lover, someone whose heart speaks to your heart. The world needs more dating. It's true that some people have bad ideas about how to date, or bad ideas about what dating means, but on the whole it's a great way to get to know someone.

For the sincere, this begins with opening yourself to living a life in the way of Jesus—a life of constant, creative prayer and utter unselfishness, a God-shaped life. Do not, in the inevitable excitement that comes with falling in love or discovering someone new, quickly throw yourself upon her. In such a hasty giving, you will lose yourself. Purity runs deeper than sexual chastity: it summons your whole personality. In love, your greatest gift is the gift of yourself. And what gift is hastily thrown together or scattered? If you are called to marriage, you must gather yourself. You must become somebody. You must pray and you must be patient about your relationships. I have seen relationships that are richly eminent, like a kind of art—usually among the elderly. They are more like a sonata than that whirligig ride most of us mistake for a "relationship"; that is, they have been built up over time, composed, carefully and sometimes painfully ordered. They are not carelessly concocted in a heat of passion or enthusiasm. Rather, they are unions that have set two broadly delineated personalities adjacent to one another, side by side, in partnership.

As I said, Christian marriage is a conversation that can lead to authentic life transformation. As a spouse, you are dedicated to help an-other hear and follow the transforming love of God, to help another attend and respond to the God who is everywhere and in all things. Christian marriage takes normal life, its sometimes busyness and sometimes boredom, and centers it on the healing of the soul. Here a man has tied himself to a woman, and a woman to a man, for a lifetime of working out salvation. Here is a unique place for the Holy Spirit to initiate and fuel a restoration in two human persons. And its fulfillment is the image and likeness of Christ. Christ will shine through each person. As a spouse the gift you have to offer is your presence and attentiveness to your beloved's life. You must not forget that the marriage knot is also a summons for you yourself to grow in relationship with God. And this begins not with throwing yourself onto each other, but in spread-out solitude and prayer. You yourself must become somebody.

For this reason, finding a spouse sometimes really begins not with dating at all, but with building rock-solid friendships, with stepping into deliberate solitude.

But you can't stay there long.

You can't be lazy with the gifts God has given you. If you are not called to celibacy, you cannot tarry in the sundry distractions of bachelorhood forever. You must eventually date—not date as the world dates (for immediate gratification of need and for pleasure), but as one learning to become somebody. Date as one who labors to build something beautiful.

Dating is fun, but for the Christian it isn't about just having fun. When God made Adam and Eve, God made something solid, something far more meaningful than a summer fling. Generally speaking, in dating you are out to discover more about yourself, what you're looking for in the opposite sex, how relationships work in general, yes; but more specifically, Christian dating is ultimately about finding a spouse, an ally in battle.

So often when Christians apply the beautiful mystery of one flesh to dating, they suddenly get serious and surreal. They start drafting structures for how it's all supposed to work, about how a relationship ought to grow in carefully coordinated stages. I've read several Christian books about dating in which the authors build a pyramid diagram for how couples ought to "grow into" one another:

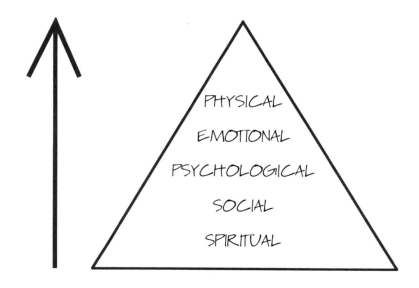

The idea is that, ideally, intimacy will grow in these stages. It starts with a spiritual connection, which carefully grows and grows, socially and psychologically and emotionally, eventually culminating in marriage and, finally, sex. Growing up in church, I saw hundreds of these diagrams, all gridding the same scheme for how to date like a Christian. For me, a serious problem with these ideologies is that, in an effort to emphasize the importance of sexual purity, they put sex at the top, as the final culmination of love. But the fact is, sex isn't the highest and best of what marriage and relationship are all about. It's up there. But it isn't the thing itself. The basic problem with these courtship schemas is that they are invented in fantasyland. No real relationship looks like what the chastity books make relationship out to be. Instead, I think human relationships look something like this:

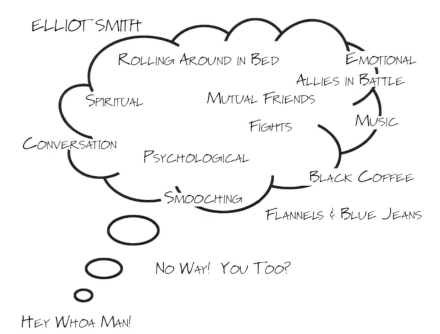

ELLIOT SMITH

ROLLING AROUND IN BED   EMOTIONAL
ALLIES IN BATTLE
SPIRITUAL   MUTUAL FRIENDS
FIGHTS   MUSIC
CONVERSATION
PSYCHOLOGICAL
BLACK COFFEE
SMOOCHING
FLANNELS & BLUE JEANS

NO WAY! YOU TOO?

HEY WHOA MAN!

It's all mixed up and tangled together—like everything else in real life. Relationships rarely happen the way we plan on them happening. Love is organic. You learn it on the field, not in the classroom. In building toward a marriage you are building a ministry, and like any ministry, it's about more than the handbook. It's about giving the gift of your self to another self. Throw out the rule books, and start studying the personality of Jesus in the Gospels. Let the creative, poetic, Semitic thought patterns of Christ get into you. You will learn how to begin loving like a human, how to begin loving like God.

And start dating. Don't get caught up in reading book after book about it all. Don't worry about the order of operations and the how-to's. Avoid anything that sounds as if it was made in fantasyland and step out into the world. Relax, be creative, and have fun. And above all, be patient. Do not rush into serious relationships. A good love is an un-rushed love.

So the first step to Christian dating is to actually find someone to date. It helps to go places where you can meet girls. In this matter I am not a good example. When it comes to finding a date, I'm not much of a winner. I don't try as hard as I could. I don't wolf whistle from my car window. I don't go out to clubs or bars with a roving eye. I just don't go out of my way to meet cute girls. But if I did, I imagine that the best places to meet cute girls would be at suburban mega churches, grocery stores, Target, art galleries, libraries, or maybe even Facebook. There's probably no limit to where beautiful dates can be found. The point is: you need to start looking; you need to start dating.

step 2: date

And yet, with all this said, whenever I think of how to date, I can't help but think don't date. So often dating is nothing more than an exaggerated claim on another person. But if you are single, you are solely God's. You can have friendships, like celibates. But no one should be able to exact from you that which you ought not give. Only in marriage are we allowed to devote ourselves so severely to someone other than God. Dating, it seems to me, is a dangerous habit that we develop through adolescence and young adulthood that commits ourselves, again and again, to a string of people.

Yet, at the same time, beginning to grow a relationship pointed toward marriage demands laying the foundations for fidelity, which requires dating and the risk of intimacy. And I don't really know what kind of specific advice to give for dating. I guess it's good to be asking the right questions. Do you have the same priorities? If you want to begin building toward a future home and career goals and your sweetheart wants to make enough money so that he/she can party this weekend, it's probably a good sign that your priorities differ. Do you respect the person you're dating? Without respect, there's no way to create a solid foundation for a deep and strong relationship. When you respect someone, trust multiplies, communication improves, and the commitment to the relationship can deepen. Another good question to ask is, Do your friends and family see what you see? If the people who love you and know you the best are dubious of your new beau, that person may not be the one for you. It's good to bring your date to visit your parents. It's good to socialize with your friends. What does this person bring out in you? Is the mundane suddenly interesting? Are you happier? Holier? More responsible? Do you manage conflict well?

Apart from asking these types of questions, I have only a few principles about dating. The best relationships are those steeped in conversation. Forget all about the virtues of playing hard to get or being aloof. You're trying to get to know somebody. Conversation is the lifeblood of good relationships.

Smooching is also important.

So is shared time.

But mostly, talking. Talking is what dating is all about. I recently dated a girl named Ilana. We went to Broadway Pizza right off Broadway and West River Road, ordered our pizza to go and drove to this beautiful spot where you can see the Mississippi and the whole Minneapolis skyline. We ate pizza in the bed of my truck, looking out at the city lights. I brought a case of Rolling Rock along, and a pack of Camels, and extra sweaters and mittens. Ilana is an atheist who loves architecture and Rilke and Mason Jennings, and I love how she's always full of interesting and unexpected ideas. We talked until every Rolling Rock had been emptied, every Camel in the pack smoked, and every last sweater and mitten donned in the late-night cold. She told me about why she doesn't believe in God and I told her about why I don't believe in Gravity. I drove her home at one in the morning. It was a very good time. I had fun and I learned a lot. If I could sum up dating with a word, it would be Conversation. Conversation is what dating is all about.

step 3: get married or break up

Breaking up is hard business. Besides the classic "It's not you, it's me" line, there are so many ways people break up: in person; via text message, carrier pigeon, Post-it note; or by doing nothing. In Minnesota, we usually initiate our breakups with common Minnesota phrases like "If it's not too much trouble . . . ," or "Ya know . . . ," or "So, the weather . . ." No matter how you do it, breaking up is bad times. There's just no way around it.

I think for Christians, every relationship eventually leads to a breakup or an engagement. Cohabitation just isn't an option. You can't date forever. And at some point in your love story you recognize either that you need to spend the rest of your life with this person or that you don't and you need to break up.

Some people think God is a matchmaker. Whenever I go steady with a girl, I'm told that if she's the one God has planned for me, it will just work out. Whenever the relationship starts crumbling, I'm told she's probably not that special one. Whenever it's all said and done and I'm really lonely, I'm told not to worry: God still has organized and scheduled a spouse for me, "the one for me," and so on. But for some reason, I am not comforted. It's not that I don't believe God can arrange marriages. It's just that I don't know if that's how he works most of the time. Love is very often something that happens to us. But it's also a decision. The kind of love to build a marriage on is a decision.

I say, forget about all of that. Be brave. When a dad gives his son paints and paper he doesn't want to color the pages himself. Not at all! He says, "Paint your heart out!" and then goes upstairs, curiously peeking down every so often to see what his boy is up to. And as long as it isn't obscene, he delights in his son's creation, hangs the pictures up on the dining room wall and pins them above his office desk. Our Lord is the same way. He's given us paints and paper and "gone upstairs." He peeks down, excited to see what we choose to make of the gifts he has given us. The last thing we should do is hang on him, always asking what he wants us to paint. What if God wants us to do the creating and the loving? What if he wants us to joyfully splash colors onto the canvas, be creative, get engrossed, make something beautiful?

Jesus once told a story about a business manager who opened checking accounts for three of his employees.[3] (Okay, I admit, I've modernized the parable of the talents.) He told them to use their business loans to start new projects and expand the company. When he later asked them how they used his money, the first one replied, "Even though it was at great risk, I invested your money. I bought and I expanded, and I have made a significant profit." The second employee also made a profit. But the third one replied, "I was afraid of losing your money, so I kept it safely in my checking account." And the way Jesus tells the story, upon hearing the third employee's reply, the manager freaks out: "You lazy rascal! You ought to have at least put my money on a certificate of deposit, so I could have got it back with interest." The manager then demands that the money be taken from him and given to the first employee who has already made a profit, "For the person who has will always be given more; and the one who has not will forfeit even what he has. Fling this useless employee out into the darkness where there is wailing and gnashing of teeth!"

Your vocation is simple. It's your job to create a beautiful love story with what God gives you. Create for God's glory. Seek God's will for your life. Follow his leading. Always lift everything up to him in prayer. But do not hang on him. Don't let fear bring you to a stalemate. Don't bury your treasure. To love is to risk. And since Christian marriage is one of God's brightest lights in a dark world, it is a risk you must take. Only you can write your love story. True, love is an unmerited gift. God himself might hand it to you. But only if you look for it.

I don't think the problem with loving is epithetic or structural. It isn't so much about your technique or method, but about learning to live well, and learning to listen. Every relationship has an inherent impossibility, which every lover quickly discovers (and usually denies) after the initial fireworks fade. She is woman and you are man, foreigners traveling a strange land, learning the other's language, surprised at how other you in fact are.

Why are we loving if not to press our hearts into the corners of life, to push its hidden meaning and possibility?

Good love is the unmaking of your mind. The beloved is always changing. Don't hold on to the old illusions. To discover and rediscover her every day will teach you how to enjoy something better than your plan, your notions of how things ought to be done, something you wouldn't have been able to enjoy ten years ago, a month ago, yesterday. Genuine relationship knows no grid or rule book. The real thing is always more difficult and wild. Empty your mind before you kiss her. You have touched only the depths of her mind, the vast world of her soul. She stands wholly apart from your plan, your idea of her. You do not know her body well enough: do not smother it with your imaginary floor plan. Go back to her, the woman with whom you fell in love, with all the newness of morning. She will be more than you knew, never less. Risk getting lost, and you find her. In the words of Kahlil Gibran on the beloved: "She became a book whose pages I could understand and whose praises I could sing, but which I could never finish reading."[4]

And so, if you love a woman—marry her. God probably wants you to.

But still, what a high summit, a Heroic Marriage. I myself find scant supplies for the journey. I am moody and restless and guilty. From any angle I look at myself, I seem unto myself . . . grizzly. Nonetheless, for this conjugal quest I have procured and gladly offer the following:

> A sturdy twin mattress; the frame stowed safely away so that it might rest flat on the floor, fashionably.

A worn copy of both E. E. Cummings's poetry, a constant companion and guide, and the Song of Solomon, which cat-naps faithfully by my low-set bedside.

A spatula. Though I am sometimes scorned for my poor dish-washing, I am joyful in all things Breakfast and Cocktail Hour.

Red silken underwear, for both comfort and foxiness.

A paintbrush.

The Great American Novel. I'm writing it in outbursts.

A debt to income ratio of 8 to 1.

A guitar, over which one can warble ballads.

Slim-cut jeans, a pair of strong legs, and a love of walking with both.

I am not yet bald or boring. I have a mane of red hair that neither falls nor flows. It's an unruly thing, but you may learn to love it.

10

Brown Like Bourbon

Let him kiss me with the kisses of his mouth!
For your love is better than wine.

—SONG OF SOLOMON 1:2

always winter, never christmas

Christians should not only work hard, but party hard. And by party I mean the whole operetta—music and dancing and eating and drinking. Clear away any idea of the tea party or coffee klatch. The picture I want you to have in your mind is dustier, more organic, and merrier. Think of a pig roast or a tailgate party, a barn dance, or an all-out hoedown. Think of Irishmen in Irish pubs hammering their pint glasses and singing boisterously. Think of farmers making the table groan from the weight of their harvest yield. Think of something like a medieval festival. These pictures are vastly different from the typical office party or church potluck. But they are the kind of pictures we should have in our minds when we think of Christian joy.

Looking around, I feel like we live in a Narnia where it is "always winter and never Christmas." Draped about us hangs either an apocalyptic seriousness or a teetotaling bashfulness. It isn't necessarily something you are doing or I am doing: it's just there, like bad background music. I can't quite ignore it. Thanksgiving arrives, and despite the plenty, I don't know how to really, truly give thanks. Christmas comes, and despite all the grandeur and lights, I cannot genuinely rejoice. Fourth of July fireworks cannot stir up within me even the mildest form of patriotism. I want to celebrate, but I often can't just let go and dance. And I don't think I stand alone. It is hard to find a joyful Christian today—a Christian who dreams and dances and makes merry. But I can't point any fingers: I am as melancholic as the rest of them.

But a somber Christian is a dangerous Christian. Or in the words of Francis de Sales, "A sad saint is a sorry sort of saint." Christ did not come preaching gloom and doom: "I came that they may have life, and have it abundantly."[1] When the sick are healed, and when the slave is set free, the only appropriate response is joy.

And as far as I can tell, real joy is never abstract or solitary. Festivity is as physical as the Incarnation and as communal as the Trinitarian life. Genuine joy is embodied joy. It naturally branches out into friendship and family and church. It must be spoken, touched, and smelled. The ancient Hebrews celebrated God with the lute and the harp and banging cymbals, with wine and folk dancing. We too should tune our banjos, fill the icebox with beer, set our jaws, and dance. The heartbeat of the kingdom is deep, spontaneous praise. The Lord's Supper is, after all, the eucharistia, the meal of thanksgiving. Of all people, Christians should be the most awake, the most carefree and full of laughter. Love, thanksgiving, rejoicing; compassion, forgiveness, a kind of patriotism for the kingdom—these are the essence of a good party.

They are also the essence of Christ.

They are also the essence of Christian romance.

We need a good stiff drink, a poetry reading, and a fresh appreciation for Sunday mornings. Artistic creation, dance, ritual, and song capture the human soul in a way the practical working world cannot. Festivity touches our transcendence. Human beings are not merely the crest of the animal kingdom; they are just "a little lower than the angels."[2] We have legends in our blood. We are in the wake of mythmakers, prophets, and poets. The implications of the Incarnation still pound through space and time. And if we are brave enough, if we believe—really believe—we will do more than move mountains: we will image forth the Light of the world.

I have heard a poetry for the practical man and woman, the working husband and wife. In some editions it's even printed in red letters, which is fitting because it hits the palate like a cool red lager after a long hot day. Although this poetry is now mostly read by self-defined nonsmokers and teetotalers, when we approach the text as it stands naturally, we can still hear the original verse narrative. And it sounds like the commotion of a late-night bar song in Dublin on Saint Patrick's Day, except holy. It is an invitation to rejoice.

Something in Christ was of blood and thunder. There was something he had to safeguard while he walked through our tiny hamlets and back roads; "some one thing that was too great for God to show us when He walked upon our earth; and I have sometimes fancied that it was His mirth."[3]

o   o   o

I bring all this up because I think that joy is the essence of Christian sexuality. Today this cannot be stressed enough. Savvy-bachelor sex and the tyranny of technique are stifling compared to the engaging and personal sex God intended. Before whatever else it might be, I think Christian sexuality and romance is lionhearted and laughing. It is a celebration.

Though I hated it at the time, one of my favorite childhood memories is of the mornings before my dad would go to work. Just as he would scramble to get out the door on time, my father would grab my mom and kiss her. My brother, sister, and I abhorred it. On some mornings, particularly Fridays, they would kiss for a long time, Dad letting the briefcase fall to the floor, Mom smiling over the moans of disapproval we would announce from over our cereal bowls. But the picture is etched into my mind forever.

"I would kiss you," says the lover in the Song of Solomon, "I would lead you to the room of the mother who bore me, bring you to her house for you to embrace me; I would give you mulled wine to drink. . . ."[4] You can hear the happiness in her eager promise. It's a kind of happiness natural to Christianity. To understand Christian sexuality in the proper light of Christ, we must first understand the Christian idea of joy. The heart of Christian sexuality is shared joy.

From early on, the church has had a cynical if not hostile attitude toward the body and sexuality. Origen, a third-century sometimes Christian thinker, held the flesh in disdain and interpreted the Song of Solomon as only allegory of God and the church. His convictions against the flesh were so strong he castrated himself. After his conversion, Augustine, a classic fourth-century theologian, equated sexuality and the body with his promiscuous pagan past. To overcome his desire for women, Saint Jerome would fling himself into thorny brambles: this method failing, he took up the study of Hebrew.

But this attitude toward sex grew out of ancient pagan dualism, which separated reality (and the human person) into two realms: spiritual and physical. The soul was of the spiritual realm and thus clean; they body (and sexuality) was of the physical realm, and thus unclean. But the Bible is very clear that as beings created in the image of God, we were designed to be body and soul together. Sexuality isn't the incarnation of sin, but the fruit of a fully human life.

This kind of dualistic thinking goes hand in hand with the sense of sexual duty or obligation that has infected many Christian marriages. Christians often get so caught up in their duties to family, church, and ministries that they think the whole of the kingdom life—even sex—as work. But God didn't design us for work and obligation alone, especially when it comes to sex. Think about it. Christianity's last word isn't Judgment Day, but eternal joy.

For the Christian, sexuality is inseparable from marriage, and marriage begins with a wedding, and (in my opinion) weddings are one of the best excuses for a party.

sex, and the importance of bourbon

The world is sin stained. But we mustn't replace hedonism with moralism. If I were to say the goal of my one-year vow of celibacy was to outline "Seven Steps to Godly Romance," any sensible person would yawn and put this book down without remorse. There seems no end to pyramid diagrams, charts, and imposing sophistries preaching the how-to's of holiness in love. To find lasting and fulfilling love, one cannot simply go through the steps of a formula as if solving a math problem. Love is not algebra.

To focus on restraint, boundaries—"How far is too far?"—can make abstinence a synonym for holiness. But I think this is a hazardous reversal of terms. A negative replaces a positive. And, as a general rule, when a negative word or phrase is used to describe a thing, we leave the issue more involved than it is naturally.

Here's a metaphor to help me explain what I'm trying to say. If we were to define an Englishman negatively, for example, "He is neither a Frenchman nor a German," we would not have defined "Englishman" at all. Definition by exclusion is infinitely complex and indistinct, for our Englishman is equally neither Chinese nor Sudanese. Definition by affirmation, however, is less mistakable. It defines an Englishman as a native to England, who shares the culture, language,

and assumptions common throughout his land. Similarly, no one, pre-
sumably, would maintain that a Christian is defined solely as "one
who denounces the devil" (negatively), but rather, as one who at least
believes in the lordship of Jesus Christ. A Christian is not best defined
negatively but positively; that is, not by what he or she abstains from
but by what he or she participates in. And herein lies the central point
of the matter. Because rule books focus on abstention, they cannot be
enough to define holiness—even holiness in sexuality.

A good way to illustrate the problem with a lot of the bad ideas
Christians have about sex is to compare them with the bad ideas a lot
of Christians have about bourbon. Here is a passage from a beautiful
poem about godly sexuality from the Bible: "Let him kiss me with the
kisses of his mouth!" writes the poet of the Song of Solomon. "For
your love is better than wine."[5] Wine, then, is the choice metaphor
for the fragrance of sexual love. The woman finds her lover strongly
intoxicating, even more so than wine. But who can fully grasp the
import of the poetry, let alone the experience, if they're rule-book-
thumping teetotalers?

The surface simplicity of the Song of Solomon is also its deep
meaning. It doesn't take a lifetime of study and scholarship to vali-
date the basic meaning of the poem legible to all Christians. When the
poet sings that love is like wine, the poet is saying that love is like the
best things in life: a good party, good company, shared joy. One of the
most mysterious, beautiful books of the Bible is laid open before us to
understand, and we will miss the message of the first chapter if we let
Christian pop culture shape our understanding of the Christian idea
of wine—to wit, Christian joy. But the firstfruits—the best vintage,
the deepest joy possible—is what Song of Solomon is all about.

It is important to point out that the poem continues, "Because of
the fragrance of your good ointments, your name is ointment poured
forth."[6] It wasn't only physical. I think the word "name" entails the
beloved's whole character and reputation. The woman was attracted
to her beloved's reputation for godliness. It is from his holiness that

she finds a joy, the kind of joy that can be likened only to fine wine, dancing, embodied celebration.

○   ○   ○

Sadly, I have seen in my life that few people inside the church learn how to laugh and dance, drink whiskey, and celebrate life and God. It is something we tend to learn outside the church and then bring back into it. When talking about festivity, or a Eucharist for that matter, one can't get far without addressing wine. In human history wine is the oldest and most fixed accompaniment to joy.

Bad religious ideas about chastity are a lot like bad ideas about bourbon. I suspect no matter how much I might emphasize righteousness and maturity with regard to drinking alcohol, some readers will still forge me into a naive and flippant tippler. Yes, we are called to live with not even a hint of impurity. Little is worse than a sloshed freshman toasting immoderation by quoting Paul's words that a little wine is good for the stomach, or by citing how Jesus turned water to wine. But we mustn't construct spiritual fictions. The Christian Way is neither total indulgence nor complete abstinence. It is a way of discernment and holiness, the narrow way. When I speak of beer or bourbon or wine, I intend absolutely no condoning of drunkenness or disreputable behavior. One can be prudent without being prudish.

My quarrel isn't with rules and structures, but with the idolatry of rules and structures. We must never think Jesus proposed only abstract theories and not rules. He wasn't a romantic visionary. The moral life he calls us to isn't a grandiose picture, something no one could ever really live out. It is practical. It is a rule. And it is doable. If the difficult demands of Christian morality are turned into tepid tenets and never taken seriously, obeyed as actual rules for living, we will only become pharisaical and jaded.

Christ loves a good life, not good ideas about living.

Moralism and bartering have no place in the kingdom. When the Holy Spirit flowers within us, takes us by storm, there is little need for dikes and levees. Just as rivers flow into the sea, the soul baptized into Christ is drawn to Christ and to his righteousness. When God's people are gathered together, joy and thanksgiving and awe are inevitable. Food and drink, the harvest table and wine, have been linked with celebration since the beginning of history. Why let the world take what is naturally good and turn it into something for back alleys and speakeasies? Pascal puts it well in his *Pensées*:

> Too much and too little wine.
> Give him none, he cannot find truth;
> Give him too much, the same.[7]

The same goes for Christian sexuality. The Christian idea of holiness in sexuality is first defined not by abstention but by indulgence. Ecclesiastes unabashedly urges "Enjoy life with the woman whom you love all the days of your fleeting life which He has given to you under the sun; for this is your reward in life."[8] And in Proverbs: "Let your fountain be blessed, and rejoice in the wife of your youth. As a loving hind and a graceful doe, let her breasts satisfy you at all times; be exhilarated always with her love."[9] "Sustain me with cakes of raisins," says the beloved. "Refresh me with apples, for I am lovesick."[10] Shouldn't we blush? Raisin cakes were considered to be aphrodisiacs, where the "seeds" could increase the "seed" of the couple's conception. Apples, like pears and especially pomegranates (ripe, seed-filled, red in color), were metaphoric of the genitals, the whole fruitfulness of the beloved's body.

Godly romance does not fit into a seventeenth-century corset, nor does it march to a twenty-first-century courting regime. If anything, it is wearing a sundress and dancing.

○ ○ ○

The hoax of hell is that God is holding something back; that the law is intended to restrict our happiness. He has indeed set up clear and distinct boundaries, fences we ought not jump, but they are the fences of a playground;[11] they are intended for our own pleasure and for our own good.

Like schoolboys who cling to the fence during recess and fail to see the swings and slides, by reducing holiness to what it forgoes, we fail to see what it delights in and guards jealously: sexuality at its best.

the poetry of a kiss

Allow me to identify two potential problems. First, fence gazing is a preoccupation with the world outside the playground, a keeping up with the Joneses in reverse. Whatever they do, we make a point not to do. If their slides are red, we'll paint ours blue. The problem is that fence gazing modifies worldly paradigms of romance, rather than expounding on the paradigms of romance God has already given us. But if we overemphasize what we are not to do, we can only denounce divorce rather than endorse marriage. Like a hearth without a fire, the kingdom life would be all morals and no mirth. Jesus offers us wine and we would be gurgling tap water. We would be paddling about in ponds when we could be manning ships at sea.

The second problem is that clinging to the fence might very well border on idolatry. When rule books are drawn up, odd regulations, practices, and rituals often arise. These resemble something like a "Chastity Cult," where young people sing songs, wear rings, march hand in hand under a banner of "courtship," and will not kiss until they walk down the aisle. No sensible person would actually maintain that sexual purity is a condition of salvation ("all have sinned and fallen short of the glory of God"). But the implicit message seems to be that those who do not wear the rings or court are less Christian than those who do. If we do indeed mistakenly equate abstinence for holiness, we could very well mistakenly come to view sex itself as inherently holy, in which case the focus would become first not God, but an idea of purity. I have heard of couples who pray before making love, as a priest would before entering the Holy of Holies. Implicitly, sexuality is put on a pedestal fit only for gods.

The secular times we live in seem to hold no regard for the propriety and modesty our grandparents took for granted. A Free Sex ideology caricatures love into something at best sentimental; or takes sex far too seriously, deifying it with superlatives as the highest and best human experience. The call to purity in the church is essential. But while the world worships sex by indulging, we must not make the mistake of going to the other extreme and worship sex by abstaining. We would all be guilty of giving sex undue reverence.

I am not for a moment attempting to discount marital fidelity or premarital purity. I am suggesting that rather than organizing our relationships around the rules of chastity, Christian lovers should emphasize the figure of their faith—that "luminous figure of the Nazarene," as Einstein called him. Law and gospel are indeed inseparable. Jesus did not come to jettison but to fulfill the law. But the pursuit of sexual holiness via the rulebook is not the same thing as the pursuit of God. The pursuit of God, however, implies holiness. If we're too busy playing on the playground, we won't even bother running to the fence.

We need imagination. And in the shadow of a secular age, perhaps we need something like what the late conservative thinker Russell Kirk called the "moral imagination."[12] Boundaries have their place, but they are not the thing itself. Godly romance cannot be reduced to methods, as if it were a natural science.

I have heard it said that if we describe a kiss scientifically, it sounds sickening: sphincter muscles tighten so as to draw the flesh around the oral cavity into a bulbous mound, and press up against another moist, creased oral cavity and exchange saliva and breath. It takes imagination to see the poetry, the beauty, of a kiss.[13] In the same way, it takes imagination to see the poetry and beauty of godly romance.

It is not enough merely to go through the motions, as if love were marked by predictability and ran by the clock. In the words of Rollo May: "The lover, like the poet, is a menace on the assembly line."[14] I love this poem by E. E. Cummings, who knew it well and says it best:

> who pays any attention
> to the syntax of things
> will never wholly kiss you[15]

We usually think of syntax as a set of rules. But, interestingly, the word comes from the Greek *syntaxis*, which combines *syn*, meaning "together," and *tassein*, meaning "arrange." Rather than emphasis on rules, the older, more important idea of syntax is one of arrangement, how things fit together to create something beautiful. And this is what the Christian idea of sex and marriage is all about.

We do not need a formula for love. Sermons outlining and graphing such are bathetic and beyond a pastor's bailiwick. Love's language is too domestic, too sexual, and too human to be reduced to three-point steps and plotted diagrams. I must learn to approach romance on its own terms. The human heart responds to parable and thinks in metaphor, not bullet-point outlines and pyramid diagrams. We must take the bricks and mortar of the kingdom and work to build a romance founded not on the sands of boundaries, but on the Cornerstone of Christendom. We could kiss dating good-bye, and kiss courting on her royal hand. We could also kiss the woman we love and tell the methods and rulebooks to kiss our backsides.

That Christian marriage is a covenant bound up in law is, or at least ought to be, a Christian given. That Christian marriage can be enchanting, delightful, sweeter than honey, is not so obvious. That Christian marriage can be sacramental and sends us on a voyage of discovery, eludes us. Springtime comes. If not holding books, sweethearts hold hands while making their way to the coffee shop or the park to kiss and be kissed back again, and we don't use the vocabulary given us to understand how this is the way God would have it. Romantic love is part of God's redemptive work.

I suppose from the outside it might not look at all "Christian" with kisses, bourbon, and dancing and all. But it is more than a love of beauty, a chorus of loud laughter, poetry, and a string of days where you cannot help but pray. God is in it. The only reason we can't see it is that we have fallen for the greatest spoof of our day. We don't expect to find God in romantic love because we have either turned romance into a moral gymnastic or denied its legitimacy. We miss the poetry, the meaning, of a kiss.

11

When Kings Go Out to Battle

I could not love thee, dear, so much,
Lov'd I not honour more.

—RICHARD LOVELACE

sin boldly

Yesterday James and I met at the Wienery again. They serve breakfast all day long, which seems to fit a cold, overcast, autumn day. It's still Ordinary Time. The colors are brilliant gold. As I drove there I left my car window cracked so I could feel the clean, brittle air. We wore wool sweaters with flannels over them, and James sported his favorite (ridiculous) hat with huge earflaps. Over eggs and hash browns I told him that I had recently read about Martin Luther's brilliant advice: Sin boldly!

"This seemed like good advice," I mused, "especially when it comes to sexuality." And then I explained to him what I meant. When

I was in high school I went to a lot of Bible studies. I spent a great deal of time during my adolescent years with other disheveled guys gathered in circles to pray and read and talk. And the conversation always—always—ended up being about masturbation: some young bloke inevitably wanted to talk about girls (which meant he really wanted to talk about his struggles with pornography and lust). I eventually stopped going to Bible studies.

It wasn't that I was an exception to every young man's battles. It wasn't that I was tired of confessing the same sins week after week (I clandestinely liked having everyone pat me on the shoulder in condolence). It wasn't even that I was only disgusted by my sin. The reason I stopped going to Bible study was because I was disgusted with my sins being so . . . well, easy; so cheap. And every week's therapy session was just a reminder that I was neither brave enough to be truly righteous . . . nor really evil. I was splashing in a kiddy pool—you know, the little plastic tubs in backyards that toddlers romp in. A kiddy pool is not only too shallow to really submerge but also too small to really swim. I was just sitting there, splashing and floundering with myself in a kiddy pool. I wasn't brave enough to pursue actual holiness, and I wasn't brave enough to actually sin. I wasn't out wooing women and making love with indigenous abandon. I stayed at home all by myself living in fantasyland.

"Sin boldly," I say, "or don't sin at all."

At least then you won't be deceiving yourself; at least then you are honest. Masturbation is like splashing in a kiddy pool; making love to a real woman is like swimming in a wide ocean. Many young Christian men just don't have the guts to get out of the kiddy pool and kiss a girl, so they resign themselves to their laptops and pillows. But it's the little sins that end up snaring you. In our secret lives, behind our bedroom doors, sin wraps its cold fingers around our hearts. You must be brave to live honestly. Love Christ either with a whole heart, or not at all. Either sin boldly, or don't sin at all. But don't settle for the easy, and the easiest end of the easy.

James agreed. And then he told me something I wasn't expecting to hear. He told me that, even though he's engaged, he still struggles with masturbation and pornography, and that nothing seems to change. It's as if we turn twelve and begin to wish upon a falling star that we would magically change so that we wouldn't struggle with the same old sexual sins. And yet we continue to do that which we do not want to do.

James's story reinforces why I believe you are living your marriage now, even if you're not married. I understand the sensualists of old, who slept with women and wrote bad poetry about it over bad wine. But I do not understand Christian masturbators. I knew three Christian men in high school who are now married. They were all holy and good—except for when their pants were around their ankles and their Internet connections strong. They started a club, where they would confess to one another; and for every time one of the poor boys stumbled, they would deal him a corresponding punch in the abdomen. It didn't work. Eventually, quietly, they accepted the defeated idea that "Maybe when I get married, all of this will go away." They're all married now. But one of them recently confided in me that they've started—all three of them—a pornography accountability club. Getting married didn't magically change them. What you do today is what you will do tomorrow. You are living your marriage now.

A lot of it is the Yoga Truth. Nothing changes if nothing changes. We might often think about righteousness, but we rarely start living it. But then, maybe it isn't so simple. Not only do humans have a hard time sticking to our resolutions, we have difficulty stopping our sinning if we focus only on the negative. In order to stop masturbating or looking at porn, you need to replace that time and energy with something wholesome and good. And this becomes all the more evident and beautiful the more you understand how your sexuality is a part of who you are as a person—as a man or a woman made in God's image—and how your sexuality can be a part of God's songs.

when men left home

I want every part of my life to be Christ's—even my sex life. I want to know how to make sex and romance into something other than road-blocks that keep me from the life Christ wants for me. I want to know if it's possible to have my sex life play a significant role in working out my sanctification. But my sexuality is uncharted territory. I think the same is true for every man, more so than for women.

Men and women are not the same. This idea rightly bothers some, perhaps because each sex has been flagrantly stereotyped in the past: the man who has to conquer nature and every woman within reach; the woman, faint and unable to take care of herself. But to cancel out these silly and suffocating stereotypes of masculinity and femininity we must not simply go to the other, homogenizing extreme by saying men and women are "the same." We are not the same. We are differ-ent, but not different in the traditional, stereotypical ways. It isn't that man is active and woman is passive. We are each active and passive in our own ways.

Sex is a beautiful picture of the rhythm and relating between man and woman. A woman comes at things on a curve; the man in a straight-on attack. There is the approach, the entrance, the union; then partial separation, and reunion. This entrance and union, with-drawal and distancing, this courtship, exemplifies the differences in the sex roles that brings out the best in men and women.

Male sexuality is nomadic, sporadic, and random. A man just doesn't understand his erection, his deep impulses, his potency. He lies with a woman. His seed reaches into the future in the life that is consummated. In some abstract way, he himself lives on in his poster-ity. But beyond insemination, he has no further direct physical con-nection with the child before it is born. Even after it grows, he is not exactly necessary for the nurturing and raising of the child. The child does not grow in his belly or suckle at his breast. "If he leaves, the family may survive without him. If she leaves, it goes with her," says

George Gilder, I think insightfully. "He is readily replaceable; she is not."[1] God does not make homogeneous human beings. He makes men, and he makes women. Socially and even strictly biologically, a man's sexuality is very different from a woman's. And I am beginning to wonder if the difference runs much deeper than sex roles but is a difference in outlook. Men are just woven from different sexual cloth than women.

I'm not very traditional in the matter of sex roles. I don't think women belong in the kitchen or at home any more than I think men belong in the kitchen or at home. From time to time I even dream of marrying a breadwinner—a lawyer or a doctor, say. She'd come home from a hard day's work, passionate about her calling, full of stories, and I'd have dinner waiting for her. I like to cook. I like to listen to Bing Crosby or Stan Getz and João Gilberto, and sauté something creative, something laced with garlic and covered in olive oil.

To be honest, between painting and writing and making music, I couldn't be happier than being left at home. Besides loving to cook, I like kids, or at least the idea of kids. I want to look out at them over the dinner table, listen to them laugh and whine and talk, and watch them hide their broccoli in their napkins. I want to play with them and discipline them and read them stories about Rastafarians and Israelites before they go to bed. The important thing to me is that family stays more important than the accumulation of stuff. What else do we live for if not for our families? Why would I rather have the new Lexus or the new hi-fi, sci-fi, plasma titanium television? It is not warm. It does not need love. It cannot love me back.

It was a sorry turn when, as a widespread phenomenon, men began to leave their homes to make their living in the city. Up until the late nineteenth century, most people in Western culture lived on small family farms. For almost all of human history, sex and marriage have been tied to the farm. And on the farm each sex held its own accomplished and satisfying sector in domestic life—for the men, tilling crops and machinery maintenance; for the women, raising the children and preparing the food—which the other would honor and respect. Life was a joint effort. It was a hard life, but it was a familial life. Urban industrialism, however, took men away from their homes. For the first time, domestic work was viewed as less progressive and less important than the distant and increasingly specialized world of professionalism. Fatherhood became abstract. A man was to provide the money, little more. His life and work were no longer wed. He lost his coherent role in the family life and has since been struggling to understand his masculinity.

But women also suffered. Marriage and family were no longer the shared life they used to be. Processed foods and laborsaving devices that removed much of the art, and much of the dignity, from her role as mother left her at home to manage menial household tasks. It's no wonder feminism has so often encouraged women to break into the professional world. Domesticity has become boring. Even a woman's role as child-bearer and mother has been taken out of her hands and into those of specialists, usually men. Women no longer give birth in the home.

The result of all this has been a growing chasm between men and women and an unappreciative view of the family. I wish men had never left domestic life. I wish women had never been restricted to it. Let us put a scissors to all those yarns we weave in public schools and in our hearts that respectable work is segregated from the place and people we love, from the home.

I belabor the point so you know where I stand on the subject of stereotypical sex roles. But with all this said, I still think women's sexuality is very different from men's. Men and women are not the same. And I think this is a good and natural thing.

Life waits, resides in a woman. Sexuality, childbearing and rearing are natural and inherent to her identity as a woman. Her breasts and womb affirm her role as a mother. Indeed, unless she is trying to be a man, she understands her body the way it's designed naturally.

She is a garden, a home in herself. She is geography, as Robert Farrar Capon puts it in a wonderful little book I read last winter: "To be a Mother is to be the sacrament—the effective symbol—of place. Mothers do not make homes, they are our home: in the simple sense that we begin our days by long sojourn within the body of a woman; in the extended sense that she remains our center of gravity through the years. She is the very diagram of belonging, the where in whose vicinity we are fed and watered. . . . She is geography incarnate, with her breasts and her womb, her relative immobility, and her hands reaching up to us the fruitfulness of the earth."[2] For women, the sex act is naturally abiding and grounded, a vocation bound up in conceiving, nurturing, commitment, and the home. Her kingdom is set in stone. Her nobility courses deep.

I myself cannot trace this mysterious territory. I can only venture into the abyss of my own masculine sexuality. For men, sex is a test of identity, a matter of exploration and accomplishment. Perhaps some form of the phallic cult broods in every society. That something, anything, to give masculine sexuality meaning, though not necessarily as pronounced as tribal initiation rites, follows men wherever they go, no matter how civilized they may be.

How are the hunters made into fathers? What steers testosterone's scattered aggression into creative and committed fatherhood? God's great commission to Adam, "Be fruitful and multiply,"[3] is etched within us, indelible. But, alike in our depravity, what God says to Cain echoes out to us as well: "A fugitive and a vagabond shalt thou be in the earth."[4] Masculine sexuality wanders and searches to understand itself. A man is a sexual nomad. Our sexuality is tied only abstractly to the family. It's almost too obscure, too intellectual and symbolic to be kept there. It tends to run off into Causes and Visions and Poetry. For men, sex is energy. If not tied down to something bigger than itself, it flies all over the place wreaking havoc. It reminds me of King David's story in the Bible.

fumbling the flowers

Listen. "In the spring of the year, the time when kings go out to battle, when David sent Joab with his officers and all Israel with him; they ravaged the Ammonites, and besieged Rabbah. But David remained at [home in] Jerusalem."[5]

Springtime is love time, as every poet and songbird knows. It's as if sex itself wakes up, rubs its eyes, and starts looking around. It's when crops are sown, new wells are dug, and "kings go out to battle."

All the vitality of David's sexuality is pounding within him, and yet he stays at home. The story continues: "It happened, late one afternoon, when David rose from his couch and was walking about on the roof of [his] house, that he saw from the roof a woman bathing; the woman was very beautiful."[6] All the energy, the energy of a lion—the springtime energy that no man can cage without killing, only harness—all this energy piles upon itself in the springtime heat, and David has no release. He chose to stay home, rather than fight with his men. And while his men fight afar, he lies on his couch, restless and bored. "So David sent messengers to get her, and she came to him, and he lay with her."[7]

> And rapidly backwards and forwards
> The early bees are assaulting and fumbling the flowers:
> They call it easing the Spring.[8]

She conceives. Backpedaling, David sends for her husband, Uriah, who is out fighting David's war for him. David asks Uriah how his friends are doing, how the war is going, and then tells him to go down to his house and "wash his feet," which is just a fancy way of saying, "make love to your wife." David hopes to cover his tracks. But Uriah doesn't go home and make love to his wife! Instead, he sleeps at the door of the king's house with the servants. David is shocked that a soldier on leave wouldn't go home to his own wife, but Uriah replies:

"The ark and Israel and Judah remain in booths, and . . . the servants of my lord are camping in the open field; shall I then go to my house, to eat and to drink, and to lie with my wife? As you live, and as your soul lives, I will not do such a thing."[9]

Desperate, David gets him drunk. But even then Uriah will not go home. He is too committed to King David and to Israel, too focused on the task before him. Finally, David secretly orders that Uriah be killed, and then marries his wife, who bears him a son. "But the thing that David had done displeased the LORD."[10]

I have read this story over and over again. Virility seems to be almost hazardous. I wonder if men simply cannot afford to have time on their hands. I wonder, if we do not focus our sexuality on something bigger than sex itself, if we'll actually miss out on what sex is supposed to be. I like the way George Gilder sees things, and agree with him. I like the way he makes us men sound like brutes, but brutes with hope. He says,

> Without a durable relationship with a woman, a man's sexual life is a series of brief and temporary exchanges, impelled by a desire to affirm his most rudimentary masculinity. But with love sex becomes refined by selectivity, and other dimensions of personality are engaged and developed. The man himself is refined, and his sexuality becomes not a mere impulse but a commitment in society, possibly to be fulfilled in the birth of specific children legally and recognizably his. His sex life then can be conceived and experienced as having specific long-term importance like a woman's.[11]

I think a man needs a lady to play the lady, that she demand he woo her, commit to her, be faithful to her, before she lets him sleep with her. In the words of Rousseau, "Her own violence is in her charms. It is by these that she ought to constrain him to find his strength and make use of it."[12] But I think that even more important (enormously more!), a man needs to dig deep into himself and face the abyss apart from her. He needs to seek God. Only then will he touch the edges of his virility, his humanity. Uriah's sexuality—which says, "I have causes, I have battles to fight: how could I sleep with my wife?"—is more complete and more wild than David's.

What I've learned from David's story is that men need tasks. John the Baptist wanders the wilderness eating locusts and honey, Steinbeck drives the back roads of America with his poodle Charley, and Father Tim tends to his flock at Lord's Chapel. The nature of masculine sexuality is that it needs ties to the future, a sense of responsibility for children, and a vital role in the family and society.

We need battles.

We need causes and poetry and vocation.

And in this way, Christian spirituality offers the best possible sex life.

o o o

The other day when I told Stephen the Philistine about Luther's idea to sin boldly he gave me a small, torn paperback of John Steinbeck's *Travels with Charley*. Steinbeck's words on violence and old age in the first chapter spur me, though—enough so that I share them with you, at length:

> I have always lived violently, drunk hugely, eaten too much or not at all, slept around the clock or missed two nights of sleeping, worked too hard and too long in glory, or slobbed for a time in utter laziness. I've lifted, pulled, chopped, climbed, made love with joy and taken my hangovers as a consequence, not as a punishment. I did not want to surrender fierceness for a small gain in yardage. My wife married a man; I saw no reason why she should inherit a baby.[13]

I feel Steinbeck is not far from the kingdom of God. This might be just because I'm young and don't want to get lost in a life of routine and comfortableness. But it also might be because his excerpt might actually set a tenor for spiritual transformation that is so often overlooked.

Steinbeck wants to see the way light and colors change, the varied American speech, the variety of smells and sounds, from the tip of Maine to California's Monterey Peninsula. At fifty-eight, he seeks adventure, not a television. In short, Steinbeck wants life, and life to the full. And this is exactly what Jesus meant when he said he came that we would "have life, and have it abundantly."[14]

Next Sunday is the Feast of Christ the King, the last Sunday before Advent. Its colors are white and gold, perfect for this late autumn season. It's a day for honoring Christ as the King of the present and future.

God's kingdom isn't sleeping. Even Father Tim in Mitford—who wants nothing more than routine and quiet, a little Wordsworth in the evening by the fire—is not allowed to roost. God just doesn't let him. Every time he sits down to catch his breath, he's called to action again. I think all hell smiles when Christians forget how to laugh and how to spit, or how to host a dinner party, or when to shout and fight for justice and love; when they abstract faith in the living God from real life itself. I believe you cannot take salvation and damnation seriously unless you take how you live your life seriously. Likewise, I believe you cannot take life seriously unless you take salvation and damnation seriously.

There is no room in the kingdom of God for timid, safe nesting.

If Jesus worked so hard at his ministry that he could be accused of working on the sabbath, and if he also celebrated life so fiercely that he was accused of being a winebibber and a glutton, then so should we. "Rejoice in the Lord always; again I will say, Rejoice," says Paul;[15] and he says elsewhere: "Whatever you do, work heartily."[16] The most striking characteristics about Christians should be their work ethic and their party ethic. Something about them should be different— more serious and yet, more playful; more loving and less needy.

As far as I can tell, Christian spirituality in its truest sense is far more overindulgent and austere than anything else on earth. Little is more alarming than a Christian who is truly Christlike.

Sadly, many Christians often recoil from genuine Christians. Holiness is not at all familiar. It is like a bomb, or a poem, or a foreign land, the one you read about all the time but have never ventured to travel into.

If domestic, it is wildly domestic.

If temperate, it is intemperately temperate.

But holiness is also never a life of extremes for the sake of extremes. It's extreme because Jesus demands of us the impossible. He wants us daily to die to ourselves, to forget ourselves, so that we might find our identity in him alone. And this includes every part of our lives; as concerns my story, even our sex lives.

12

Jesus Is Sexual

None are so old as those who have outlived enthusiasm.
—HENRY DAVID THOREAU

putting on christ

During my year of celibacy, I started to notice new facets of my sexuality. It wasn't so much that I wanted sex, but I wanted something to do; and not just something to do, but something to get engrossed in, something to live for. I learned how important it is for me not to look to sex for purpose or meaning. Masculine sexuality at its best inclines toward great quests and heroic deeds. Sex isn't about sex. It's about enthusiasm, enthusiasm for something or someone. During those quiet, single months I realized that no one else is so fully human, so fully masculine, as Jesus Christ. Even though he was single and chaste, Christ Jesus is a model for sexuality.

George Washington is reported to have said that to become a man of character one must "put on" a character, the way an actor in a play

adopts the role of a soldier or a king. Slowly, and without many immediate changes, you become Christ. His personality creeps into you and
changes you. You become "a man of character." I love this idea. If you
want to love like Christ, you must "put on" Christ. Though you don't
understand it, you must play the role, get into the character, think his
thoughts, dream his dreams, pray his prayers. Imitate Christ.

Paul wrote, "Husbands, love your wives, just as Christ loved the
church and gave himself up for her."[1] But who ever accomplished
such heights? Even the best husband would confess to stumbling in
the dark, that if it weren't for patient wives and concerned friends he
would be utterly lost. And yet, "Be imitators of God," Paul;[2] "learn
to love as Christ." The charge is there. It is a tall order. There is no
way around it. I don't think Paul would have charged us to do so if he
thought it was not possible.

Yet, as I write this, I can't suppress the thought that I do not know
what I'm talking about. I'm sitting by the radiator as I write. Freezing
snow masks the brown earth and streets of Minneapolis in a dazzling
white, and to save money my roommate and I keep the thermostat at
a frosty sixty-three degrees. I'm wearing my favorite slippers. They
make me feel like a writer. It's Christmas Season, the twelve days from
December 25 to January 5, a time for Christians to reflect on the birth
of Jesus, the Word Incarnate. And so many cliché-sounding phrases
and pop images are running through my head that I'm afraid I can't
break through to the actual person of Jesus Christ.

Be imitators of Christ, says Paul.

We must immediately forget any idea that Jesus is familiar to us,
that we understand him and what he's about. Take a step back. If
you're anything like me, you are not at all as acquainted with the story
and personality of Jesus Christ as you think you are. The intensity of
Jesus' personality jumps off the page. Here is a high-octane man of
punches who accepted no poppycock. Approach him as the stranger
he is and learn from him. He is always teaching.

Some people think that if you attribute a human quality to God, you risk making God in your own image. But I think this is a dangerous road of negations. When we read the Bible, we discover a startlingly "human" God—a God of rage, mercy, love, and community. And God is who he is. So if God displays "human" attributes, it is because humanity reflects him, not because God reflects us. I think a more important danger in Christian spirituality is to make God into something we've thought up, something like a platonic and benign First Mover. As I said before, when Jesus calls God "Father" he's not using human metaphor to help us understand how things work spiritually. I think it's the other way around. I think the Bible story tells us that God is the very definition of Father, and that all our earthly fathers are but metaphors of his true fatherhood.

Jesus is the God who became human. Not almost human. Really human. Fully God and fully man, at the same time. Christians call this the incarnation of God. While still remaining entirely God, God also became entirely human in the person of Jesus. He became 100 percent mud and 100 percent poetry. Which means that Jesus is a sexual being, just like every other human. And this is because sex is not merely about intercourse. Where did we get all our energy and need for sexual connectedness? There is something emotional, even spiritual, in our sex drives. Sex is enthusiasm. In Jesus' case, especially, sex is enthusiasm (*pazzo d'amore, ebro d'amore*, "in God"). Another word for it is zeal. And if sex is about more than sex—if it's about zeal—then I think our sex drives suggest to us that we were made for deep relationship and connectedness, the kind of connectedness we get a foretaste of in sex. I think it hints that we were made for God.

○ ○ ○

Jesus is jealously sexual. But, unlike every other man, Jesus is realistic and responsible with sex. A young man's sex drive is nearly unabated. It's more than lust. It is a question of identity and purpose. And without commitment to one woman in marriage who can offer him meaning and continuity to his deepest drives through family, children, and a regular sex life, a man will wander, indifferent to how he affirms his most primitive masculinity. The need for affirmation, to "feel like a man," the most rudimentary impulse for release, drives men to find sexual fulfillment almost anywhere. And this is because sex isn't about just sex. Why else do you think pornography is a multibillion-dollar market?

Jesus never went around pretending that he's all poetry and no mud. Jesus never denied his humanness or his sexuality. Instead, he harnessed it, redeemed it, and applied it wholly toward his purpose. Jesus' complete obedience to the Father, his undivided attention to the things of God, sawed and hammered his whole life into the shape of his vocation on earth, the Cross. Jesus demonstrated that the violence in a man, the immovable need for purpose, does not find release in sex itself, but in life as a whole, a purpose-filled life. Jesus is the source for the best life possible. He alone can satisfy our deepest needs, without which we would be incapable of genuinely loving or truly enjoying sex for what it is. When we look to Jesus we discover that male sexuality isn't about lust: it's about living a life of purpose, as a one-of-a-kind man with your own unique personality and vocation.

The apostle Paul's exhortation, "Husbands, love your wives, just as Christ loved the church," is too often repackaged into a vague notion of "selflessness." Self-less love is an oxymoron. Christ's love is not self-less. That is the last thing it is. The best love comes from a person who pours his personality, his whole self into it. Christ poured his self wholly into others, offered them all he had. "God is love," says John, and he goes on to give us not metaphysics, but a personality.

Jesus' sexuality was best illustrated in his love and dedication for his Father. Even at the age of twelve he understood his life mission on earth: "I must be about my Father's business."[3] Jesus knew who he was, and his vocation consumed him, even till his dying breath, "It is finished."[4] He would always take time apart, always go to the desert or the hills to fast and to pray and to be with his Father. And in that solitude, he found his comfort and calling. Jesus embodied celibacy, for celibacy is passionately sexual. Jesus' sexuality exploded into causes, tasks, and poetry. He was in complete solidarity with God. "Just as you, Father, live in me and I in you."[5] And his love overflows, reaches into broken lives, and makes whole. "As the Father has loved me, so I have loved you; abide in my love."[6]

I wonder what this intense and holy sexuality looked like in a world sexually bastardized and confused. For once a whole and complete man walked the streets of broken men and women. Jesus is the only whole and complete Self who, in offering himself, loves wholly and completely. His virility and zeal for his Father's house, his mission, overflows into love for the overlooked, the twisted and needy, the forgotten.

And isn't this what a woman wants? Not a sex-hungry body, but a gentle and exciting, daily growing personality to embrace her? Catherine of Siena, a medieval mystic, confessed of Jesus: "He is pazzo d'amore, ebro d'amore," or, as Brennan Manning puts it, he is crazed with love, drunk with love.[7] Jesus' love is unlike anything else on earth. He is devoted, rooted in the Father. And for this reason, his sexuality does not wander like yours or mine. It heals, completes. All love is God; "God is love," pens the apostle John. This archetypal love is open, natural, and uninhibited. Christ's self-giving, free-gift love gives without apparent external cause. And if we could but learn how to imitate Christ's model love in our solitude and in our relationships and in our marriages, we would begin to understand sex and happiness. Catherine of Siena says elsewhere: "Get drunk on the blood of Christ crucified! Don't let yourself die of thirst when you have it right there before you! And don't take just a little, but enough to make you so drunk that you will lose yourself."

Holiness is not primarily about denying something. Christian spirituality doesn't work that way. It's never about giving up and saying no for the sake of giving up and saying no. It's not about giving up and saying no to the pleasures of this world but rather reaching for Christ and saying yes to the best possible plan for our lives. The only reason we don't see that is because we think we understand Jesus.

baby blue eyes

I think that when most people think of Jesus, they picture some variation of the same blue-eyed, honey brown hair and pale skinned northern European Jesus. That picture is indelibly burned into our brains. I don't know how we know it's Jesus. Maybe it's the pseudo-biblical robes that give him away, or perhaps the neatly trimmed beard. Or maybe it's the light shining down upon his masculine, straight-jawed and virile face that somehow manages to remain romantically tender, slender—effeminate, even. Regardless, no matter how hard I try to shake this image of Jesus, I can't. It's always there, looming in my subconscious. And it invades my prayer space and spiritual life.

The Jesus most of us can't help but imagine looks like someone right out of a commercial or a street pamphlet. Our image is usually some variation of the popular picture *Head of Christ*, painted by Warner Sallman in 1941. This popular artist modeled his pictures of Jesus after wartime advertisements: an uplifted face, eyes looking slightly upward or directly at you, the theatrical lighting, the head-and-shoulders studio posture, the golden sheen of heroism and celebrity. It is an image that comes from patriotic propaganda, Hollywood film, and commercial advertising popularized in the first half of the twentieth century.

The Jesus most of us can't help but imagine is painted like an advertisement.

No wonder he seems so . . . well, un-human, so un-God.

When I read the story of Jesus of Nazareth, the last thing I want floating around in the back of my mind is a pop-culture image. Pictures of Jesus like Sallman's, which are carefully designed and marketable, turn Christ into something cliché, familiar, and unreal. It misrepresents who Christ is and what he's about.

Some people think we need to do away with pictures altogether. They say Jesus is God and God can't be captured in a single picture. But humans think in pictures. It's because we're not just made of poetry. We are mud. Whenever we pray we have a picture of Jesus in our minds, whether it's a bright white light or the felt-board cartoon from our childhoods or a Rembrandt painting. What we need, then, isn't a doing away with pictures, but a thousand pictures, pictures that paint different facets of his divinity and humanity and personality.

For a long time I didn't realize how beautiful a thing it is that Paul encourages husbands to love their wives as Christ loved the church. As silly as it is to admit, I think it's because I assumed it meant to look something like the popular pictures of Jesus. But I recently saw a dad walking into the Isles Café on Twenty-eighth Street. He was a trim, brown-haired thirty-something in jeans and an untucked, wrinkled, white dress shirt with both sleeves rolled up. His tiny daughter sat on his strong right arm, tattooed in pink and blue flowers and dragons. His son reached up to hold his father's free hand, using it as a fulcrum to swing as they walked, dragging his red rain boots on the ground. The man ordered two coffees and two orange juices, and father and children all sat at two tables down from me. His wife pulled up soon after in a small Volkswagen; she was very, very pregnant. She asked him if he'd remembered to get decaf, which he had, and if he wouldn't mind doing a great many things for her, for their son, for their daughter, about the car, about the umbrella over the table, about the napkins.

He didn't seem the least bothered.

It was as if this—the sun, his children, his wife, the spilled orange juice—was what his life was all about, as if there was nowhere else he would rather be.

Lately when I think of Jesus, I think of this man and his family. It's a strange practice I have, taping snapshots from life and art together into a collage, an eclectic image of Jesus. They help keep Jesus real and interesting to me. But despite how helpful pictures are, at the end of the day better pictures or paintings of Jesus are not the best way we can rediscover him. To rediscover Jesus we need to read the memoirs of the doctors, bankers, and fishermen who knew him. His closest students, who spent three years in close camaraderie with him, did more than document his life. He was a carpenter from Galilee. And he would walk the back roads through our hamlets and cities, and talk as if he knew the secret of life. He stepped over the threshold of our earth and ate our food and drank our wine, and he told stories of the kingdom of God and the second birth of a man, how all of life could be lived in the light of the love of God himself.

Jesus was a stranger in our midst. I imagine there was something of the fields and of children's laughter in his gaze; something tender, yes, but also something of wildfires and of censure burned in the sockets of his eyes, something that would make you want to look away, afraid. There is nothing familiar or safe about telling the religious leaders, "Destroy this temple and I will rebuild it in three days."[8] How could a man say, "I am life," or, "I am the way to God," and not be conscious of his own strength? And what man uncertain of his violence would stand up to arrivistes and gurus and say, "He who is without sin should throw the first stone"?[9]

o o o

If you're seeking a fresh look at your marriage, or if you're single and hoping to bring honor and integrity to your relationships, imitate Christ. Learn to take your sexual passion and turn it into spiritual fervor. Sex is about more than sex. And the best thing you can do to understand your sexuality (which, as far as I can tell, is a huge part of your humanity), is to open your heart to the God who is real. In him you will find rest for your soul. And he will take your heart and reshape it into something neither selfish nor restricting, but self-giving and true.

Face the dawn alone. Every man's questions, his petty sexual addictions, his looming and indefinable energy, are answered in the person of Jesus Christ. Brought into the captivity of Christ, sex is made complete.

We must, like him, go to the foothills, and in the quiet and the aloneness and the terror of stepping away from Eve, find God, and find ourselves.

This was the idea behind my year of voluntary celibacy. Sometimes we need to walk away from what we want if we ever hope to get it. I was tired of looking to Eve to meet a need only God can fill. I was not only missing out on God, I was missing out on Eve. I am constantly thinking about sex. But I was drinking from a well that, no matter how much I would drink, would only leave me thirsty. When I am honest with myself, I realize that I am thirsty for friendship with God. You were "created to be like God—truly righteous and holy,"[10] says the apostle Paul. I will never be at home with my sexuality until I bring it to Jesus.

I want to be a man—a real man, not just a phony. I want to belong to something bigger than myself. I want to walk with God the way David walked with God, even though he struggled with the same temptations I struggle with. And intimacy with God, the kind Jesus had with his Father, is a choice, not an accident. I cannot wait until I feel strong enough or confident enough. I need to move ahead in my weakness, despite my fears, and pursue Christ.

Life is not about me. This is my greatest responsibility and most immediate privilege: my life is all about fulfilling God's purpose. I will never understand and rest secure in my sexuality until I understand and rest secure in this truth.

To follow Jesus is to arrange your whole life in him and around him, almost as practically as the way some people arrange their whole life around a new job or moving to a new neighborhood. Jesus demands a whole new way of life in which he is the center, the circumference, and every point in between. "In the same way that you gave me a mission in the world, I give them a mission in the world."[11] That kind of life is a strange and beautiful adventure. And this is the best possible way to prepare for sex and marriage, because this is what sex and marriage is all about. Build an inner sanctuary. Let Christ be your first thought in the morning, and he will fill your hours, your days, your love story.

13

Buddha and a Pragmatic Catamaran

Is that dance slowing in the mind of man
That made him think the universe could hum?

—THEODORE ROETHKE

the curvature of the sun

It's July again. I paint houses in the summer, which doesn't leave me much time to write. Even if I did have the time, I wouldn't want to. I prefer to drink cold beers in my city apartment with Stephen the Philistine after hot days of painting in the suburbs. I prefer going on dates. I am, after all, a man, and one not called to a lifetime of single-ness. With the conclusion of my year of celibacy I resolved to start dating again. I have thence learned that I'm still not the perfect boy-friend. I'm proud and emotional and an idealist—a nasty combina-tion in the throes of a quarrel—and I'm absentminded. It's the Yoga

Truth. Nothing changes if nothing changes. I thought that abstinence from relationship would benefit my relationship with God and eventually my relationship with others. Honestly, I don't know if it did much to help either. Relationships are, alas, beautifully, not bound to my theories about relationships. They're better. They're real. They follow no formula. And they can teach us what we really need to know. And for me this subject is worth giving up summer beers and summer dates to write about.

There is no single way to date or kiss or live out a marriage, though there is a paramount reason why we should date and kiss and marry. We are, I am convinced, mud and poetry. On the one side we are earthy and mortal and needy; on the other, we are soul-filled and bursting with passion. Satisfaction born of both mud and poetry is one of the great gifts a relationship can afford you. Yet, even more, behind and above the immediacy of sex and marriage and friendship, is the activity of God. Why should we marry? Why make love? Why write poems and kiss girls and risk getting your heart broken? Because relationship gives you a real person, an-other. Because, if taken seriously, as a discipline, as a lifelong class, relationship is one of God's ways of drawing us into better relationship with him.

Because relationships are experimental and practical, full of error and anomaly, the question of "How?" is important. But for Christians the theoretical question "Why?" is paramount. We love because relationship prepares us for change, and the last change is universal and irreversible. We love to strengthen and broaden the self. We love to strengthen and broaden an-other self. We love because it is a way of loving God himself.

For the Christian, Jesus is the vision and the inspiration for good loving. The fulfillment of our mud and poetry waits for fulfillment in him. Christ should be the impetus behind how and why we love because he is what good loving points toward. Relationship is a discipline, something you learn. No one can master it; but we can grow in it. And here's the beautiful thing: if you become an authentic lover (husband, father, friend, boyfriend), you can become an illumination to others. You can point them—though not by any means you yourself may boast of—to the fulfillment of their own muddy, poetic hearts. A good love builds an appetite for Christ.

How shall we then learn to love? Whence are both common sense and wonder found? God is always singing, always arranging and adjusting, always telling it slant. He wants to draw us to him, to make us whole in him. This deep truth is central to Christian marriage. It's the key to romance. And it all begins with learning to walk humbly before the Lord, as a discipline; to become receptive to the activity and the voice of God in your relationships. And this receptivity is what this chapter is about.

I didn't learn any practical lessons from my year of voluntary celibacy, but I did learn that the doorway to good loving only opens with a posture toward God and life as a whole. You cannot talk about love without eventually talking about everything. What love is depends on what the whole world is. And so, for me at least, love begins with learning how to look and how to listen. Learn how to build your own Poetry Boat.

○ ○ ○

My friends and I often walk to the lakes in our neighborhood to sit by our favorite trees, talk, smoke, and read poetry. After a long day of painting houses, I join them to just sit and look out at the world, to take it all in. Sailboats glide across the horizon. Couples walk by holding hands. We daydream. Once, in a moment of great understanding, we determined to save up and buy our own little boat, a Poetry Boat. We daydream about carrying it above our heads down to the water, singing as we go, oars in hand, toting a backpack full of books and luncheon. We'd raise a mast and hoist a decorated sail. The whole idea is to spend an afternoon on a lake—sipping cold ones, reading, just listening to the music in the world, just looking out at the curvature of the sun.

The way God-light shines everywhere in the world—refracted, shining through the world at an angle—is what I like to call the curvature of the sun. There is no irrefutable argument for God. We do not see him walking down the street or dancing on the clouds. This is because God reveals himself in our daily lives the way sunlight is revealed through the atmosphere or through a prism—refracted, brightly colored, dancing everywhere. It's the curvature of the sun. On a graph, a curve is a line showing how one quantity varies with respect to another. Graphs are ugly things. But on any given day, a curve is how the mud and poetry of being human varies with respect to God. It's beautiful, like a boy and a girl making eyes at one another from across a dance floor. Our daydream of a Poetry Boat is just us gawking at God from across a dance floor. It's like a portable hermitage, a spiritual retreat, a place from which we can savor and enjoy God. Though refracted, his activity is everywhere, dancing and colorful. The curvature of the sun is the romance of God, his story in our lives and in the world.

a pragmatic catamaran man

True to form, when Stephen the Philistine heard about our resplendent ambition he scoffed and remarked that while we sit in our puny Poetry Boat, he'll happily speed by in a sleek, new, pragmatic Catamaran. Left awash in his wake, we would look after him, wet and defeated, as he sailed off into the sunset on the cool breezes of atheism and unpoetry.

Though jest and chaff, this story personifies for me something I've been thinking a lot about lately—especially with regard to romance and Christian marriage. I recently read a parable someone pinned on a café bulletin board that Buddha used when teaching his disciples: "When a finger points to the moon, wise men look at the moon whereas the ignorant look at the finger and do not see the moon, or the truth." I think this parable illustrates the way a lot of people think today. Many of us speed along in pragmatic catamarans. We see only the finger but miss what it's pointing to. We see only the prism, but never turn to see the refracted rainbows dancing all over the walls. We miss the meaning of it all. And missing the truly meaningful is dangerous to our ability to be perceptive to the world and to each other, to how God is working in our relationships.

We are increasingly confused about the mud and poetry of human existence. I sometimes wonder if we are under a dark spell, not the kind of spell that enchants and awakes, but the kind that sends boys back to bed on mornings with fresh snowfall; the kind of spell that leaves you sighing, Is that all? There's a rumor that what is real originates solely from the empirical, what I call the papier-mâché pragmatic. It's a paper-thin philosophy, and I think it has made the mud and poetry of our lives as dull as dishwater.

We today have reduced the crowning features of the human person—the capacity to reason, to love, to get angry, to show mercy—into an affair of the nerves, a chemical foxtrot. By acknowledging only what is tangible, we see rainbows as mere refractions of light through water, but miss the covenant meaning. Our forebears had chivalry and poetry. We have science and psychology. We have a rhetoric that construes romance into chemical compatibility. Disenchanted, we fail to see the divine reality and eternal consequence of our relationships. Empiricism has cast a matter-of-fact spell, a synthetic vision that turns all reality upside down.

Reality turned upside down makes the obvious obscure, and the obscure obvious. A man affirms that cigarette tar causes lung cancer and that cholesterol causes heart disease and yet denies that sin causes death. If smoking cigarettes and eating steaks were a matter of faith, as is sin, it would certainly take more faith to believe in the harm of the former than of the latter. It takes microscopes and labs to see tar and cholesterol; I need only step out into the street to see sin. This is, by no means, a logical argument. Nonetheless. When one denies sin, one's whole world is turned upside down. Darkness is mistaken for light, depths are mistaken for heights, condoms and one-night stands seem safer than common sense and fidelity. By trimming human experience down to the empirical, we marginalize the human heart. Like Stephen the Philistine, we sail into the sunset on the cool breezes of unpoetry and pragmatism.

Our upside-down worldview reminds me a little of third-century Manichaeism. In an era of paganism, Hellenism, and budding Christianity, Gnostic dualists clove the flesh from the spiritual by dividing, categorizing, and theorizing. They did so, however, in a vocabulary that could speculate which was good and which was evil. To them, the delights of eating, procreation, and children were "evil" because they were of the flesh—a "lesser" reality than the spiritual. Sex was a devilish affair, a stump one trips over when caught off guard. To the Manichaean, humans were purely soul, a spirit "trapped" in a bodily cell.

In an era of pop-Newtonian physics and pop-Darwinian biology, the pragmatic-catamaran person denies not the physical but the spiritual by dividing, categorizing, and theorizing. Passion, conscience, and love are a trick of the nerves, no more. Sex becomes nothing more than animal need, necessary for species survival or, at best, a "nightcap" before bed. A person is mere body and nothing more.

But I think sexual body and passionate heart are not merely by-products of excited nerve endings. The human person is a soul embodied: not a soul "trapped" in fleshly coils, but a soul enfleshed. We are mud and poetry. Flesh and bone mingle with heart and soul. A human person does not "have" a body because humans are bodies. A human person does not "have" a soul because humans are souls. Our hopes and fears, loves and hates, are neither by-products nor oppositions of the body, but rather part of the personal whole. Here is our quandary: if we undermine our spiritual elements, we might end up on a pragmatic catamaran and drift into waters of fabricated reality; if we undermine our physical elements, we are in danger of getting lost in the clouds. Our human vessel is a paradox we must balance lest, by rocking, we dip our toes into bad thought or worse, capsize into heresy, where we find both the Manichaean and the contemporary disbeliever.

Where the pragmatic-catamaran individual negates the spiritual, the Manichaean negates the physical, and both misinterpret the spiritual and physical phenomenon of humanity. The Christian's synthetic vision, however, is all meaning. And all facts are understood in light of that meaning.

I think all Christians are inclined toward Poetry Boats—even Christian mathematicians and scientists. Christians claim an unseen reality lies behind and within the physical. To them, the visible reveals the invisible. They don't assume that what they cannot see does not exist. They perceive both the spiritual medium and the physical and believe the higher can be translated in the lower. They have some sense that great things depend on small; "some dark suggestion that the things nearest to us stretch far beyond our power," says G. K. Chesterton, "some sacramental feeling of the magic in material substances, and many more emotions past finding out."[1]

"I wish that if God were out there, he'd be a little more obvious," sigh many of my pragmatic-catamaran friends. Here is a catholic sentiment. We would all prefer God, if there is a God, to make himself plain. Speak, O Lord, a little more clearly! Yet, as Emily Dickinson would put it, God only tells it slant. He does not simply walk down the street and greet you. He does not bombard you with irrefutable facts. His pleasure is to always withhold a little beauty and meaning, like an artist who won't explain his paintings. But he reveals it nonetheless. He isn't floating aloft and aloof in some feathery realm, as some mystics claim. If God's revelation floats above us at all, it cannot help but stir the muddy bottom. Christian theology isn't only clear and glistening. God's revelation always stirs up the sediment, and makes the whole world a beautiful brown again. God does not simply split reality into the physical and the spiritual, like an old philosopher. He is rather like a child playing in a lake, loving the warm mud between his toes.

Christians believe traces of God are always, everywhere, and in all things, present. They have neither a Gnostic denial of the earth nor an empirical emptying of the earth. The world to them is full and cannot be affirmed enough. This is because every Christian, by definition, is romantic.

what is romance?

Romance is a mud and poetry posture. It's a way of receiving the experience of life. There is the experience of beauty—the kind of beauty that demands to be articulated in some way but chokes you and leaves you stammering. You want to drink it, breathe it, swim in it, become it; yet you remain bound to the confines of your body and the limits of your imagination. Beauty is what ties together our poems and dreams, the trees and loved ones. But there is also the experience of love and joy, or awe and adoration; or even the experience of pain—the pain of a broken back or a broken heart or broken dreams; or the terrible pang of loneliness.

I believe that most experiences and things we call "romantic" are an expression of our desire for something more. It can be as grand as the Colonial American longing for freedom or as simple as the quiet, often unspoken, murmur in old men's banter over pipes and beer, sharing stories from "the good old days." Romance is the kind of ache memory feeds; the muted, heart-clenching growl of nostalgia. It is the hunger pang a child feels when he smells the aroma of brownies drifting from his mother's kitchen. Or that wish-I-were-there! pull a young man feels when he sees pictures of distant lands. Or that wish-you-were-here! tug when, in that distant land, he misses his sweetheart. The hunger, yearning, and wanderlust are bittersweet because they remind us that there are brownies and sweethearts and far-off countries—none of which are immediately accessible, but easily could be. In a way, this is what makes life worthwhile. We want the bittersweet. It is more satisfying than fullness. It's more adventurous than being content to stay at home. It makes us dream and aspire and come alive.

We don't want to lose ourselves in routine, to find nothing more beyond the alarm clocks and rush-hour traffic, economy and scheduling of daily life. Our desire for something more, for what is just around the bend, is no mere momentary discontent, as if fluffing up the pillow or adjusting the thermostat could make it disappear. Try as we might, we cannot escape it. It looks up at you from your plate, keeps you awake at night, sings when your beloved laughs, and tears you open when she cries.

Though we cannot escape it, neither can we grasp it. Every moment seems to let us down or pass us by. Those things that move us most, that touch our deepest reserves, seem to awake some sleeping tempest. The thing you want is precisely the thing you cannot get. We could search to the ends of the earth in an effort to capture the electrical current of that moment that so strongly moved us, but at best we would find no more than scattered recollections.

Something lies behind a kiss, holding a newborn, taking in a sunset. The classicist's books and the poet's poems cannot be in themselves the romance. The troubadour's wildest love affair or Wordsworth's most palpable moments in nature are but ripples of a much larger tide. The books we love and the records we listen to in our living rooms are not the thing itself. Even if you could go back and relive your first kiss or re-travel Europe, you would not find what it is exactly you remember. It wasn't in the traveling or the kisses. It only came through these things. And it was longing.

Things romantic stir up within our muddy-poetic heart's longing. Longing is the heart of romance. It is the heart of mud and poetry.

It is as if some voice springs up from the earth, holds together the planets in their orb, and sounds through our experiences. But it comes to us only in echoes and muted tones, as if shouting from across a canyon or the other side of a wall. If we think the majesty of the forest or the drama of the stage is itself the romance, we shall never understand. You have to leave the walks in the woods and the kisses behind and go back to your Bible, to prayer, to church.

Although scarred from sin, the good things on earth still bear traces of their original glory, their original purpose. They are like road signs pointing our way home. They light our path. All the love and hate, all the sickness and laughter, all the sex and first snow-flakes, all the late-night talks and dinner tables and children, poetry and storytelling—all things romantic—all are cracks for the Light of the world to shine through. They are vernacular translations of a far richer, more universal language. They are prints of the real painting, echoes of the first call.

The romance of being made of mud and poetry is not merely the silly, the head-over-heels, or the hopeless. What makes something truly romantic is if it opens us to receive what is offered here and now. Something is communicated through the story of our lives, pointing to something or Someone, stirring in us a longing without remission. It speaks to us through a beautiful alpine vista, the smile of a loved one, or a terrible loss. And it is the echo of that first Voice who spoke our world into existence calling us to himself; a summons to participation in the grand story of the activity of God, and in this vein, some have called it a sacred romance.

the drawing of the veil

I want my life to become sacramental, not necessarily in the strict sense of the Roman Catholic or Eastern Orthodox Churches; that is, relating to the seven sacraments,[2] but in the broad sense: to convey something of spiritual or sacred significance; something that is a "symbol" or "icon," an outward sign of an inward grace. Like sunlight through a stained-glass window, I believe romance is what hints at the world behind the world. "Just as you see that a ray of light entering through a window is colored in different ways according to the different colors of the various parts," says the celibate monk Bonaventure, "so the divine ray shines forth in each and every creature in different ways and in different properties."[3]

The concept is especially familiar with the Eucharist. Bread and wine are tasted, digested, and experienced as the Body of Christ. We meet God. The lines between the physical and the spiritual are blurred until indistinguishable. And this is to become our daily bread. What we receive at the dinner table should liken to what we receive in the Eucharist until every meal becomes an actual Eucharist; until the Sunday liturgy is the liturgy of the workaday, the kitchen, the bedroom. Christian romance takes the principle of the Eucharist and applies it to daily life.

We could call it the "transposition" of the supernatural in the natural or the "transubstantiation" of the spiritual in the physical, but neither of these fully captures the breadth of the mystery. Jesus wasn't an Aristotelian philosopher. He was a Jewish carpenter. And he, not our ideas, must be our starting point. For this reason, I would rather call it incarnational. Christ is the Light of the world. Christian romance sees everything in light of him. It is a room with a view, a world a man can breathe in, full of purpose and glory.

An incarnational posture toward the world is primarily the belief that God speaks to us through what he has made. The mud and poetry in us desire to look beyond the Buddha's finger, to see the moon, to see where the finger is pointing. The author of the book of Hebrews writes that faith is "the assurance of things hoped for, the conviction of things not seen."[4] And things unseen are discerned "through what has been made."[5] Science and poetry should be, not conflicting, but complementary ways of perceiving reality. To find Christ in the depths and heights and beauty of daily life we must open our eyes to the world around us for what it truly is: the stage upon which the great Wooer himself fights for our attention and love.

But our experience of beauty is always a dusting, or wiping away of the first-Fall smudge on our human glasses. "Beauty is a fearful and terrible thing!" cries Dostoyevsky's Dmitri. "Fearful because it's undefinable, and it cannot be defined, because here God gave us only riddles. Here the shores converge, here all contradictions live together. . . . Here the devil is struggling with God, and the battlefield is the human heart."[6] And I wonder if today the devil does not so much attack head-on, but carefully weaves a spell, a thin and empirical film over things.

We could go down the road of negations. We could start denying the world, rejecting all that is of the flesh. But the same Lord who gave counsel to pluck out the eye was called a glutton and a winebibber. He commands his disciples to abandon all images but himself, and then promises them a hundred times more: the final vision and enjoyment of God, an image so glorious it outweighs all negations.[7] God is in, really in, his creation—not because creation is an extension of God, as the pagans believe, but because creation speaks of him, radiates him, reflects him, "like shining from shook foil."[8] *Terra ubique Domini*, says Martin Luther. The earth everywhere is the Lord's.

Despite the vast and incomprehensible otherness of God, we cannot overlook the nearness, the presence, of God. God is love. God is justice. God is the person of Jesus Christ. These are not symbols: God is ultimate reality, and all good things are a reflection of him. Christianity does not give us platonic circles and lights. What we have before us is Baptism, the Eucharist, the Galilean, Golgotha, and a rolled-away stone. Christianity, like Judaism, is grounded in a great organic and holistic earthiness, romance. What I have before me is house painting, book writing, cleaning my kitchen, and learning to date girls better. All I have is Christ, and the prayer that he can take the little things of my life and make them into something beautiful.

○ ○ ○

We need reality to break the spell of pragmatism and unpoetry, to dust our hearts' glasses that we might see the eternal consequence of our lives. In Dante's words, we must struggle "to look once more upon the stars." We must awake, like children on fresh-snowfall mornings, if we are to ever recapture the astonishment and wonder of the world that children know so well.

Perhaps this is why Christ tells us we must have childlike faith to find him at all. All the "progress" of modern empirical thought, the notion that human beings are machine and the world a cloud of atoms, is a mess of half-truths that take all the romance, the poetry and meaning, out of life. It is the chiding, shaming voice of "common sense" that sends boys back to bed. Like flowers turning toward the rising sun, if we turn and open the poetic eyes of our hearts to see like children, to be taken aback, taken by storm, only then might we pass through the threshold and into the activity of God.

Perhaps long before conversion, every Christian has been stirred, awoken in his or her muddy-poetic heart. And the human heart longs for purpose, a world filled with meaning. "The world is charged with the grandeur of God," shouts Gerard Manley Hopkins. "It will flame out, like shining from shook foil; it gathers to a greatness, like the ooze of oil."[9] Angels sing, "Holy is the LORD Almighty; the whole earth is full of his glory";[10] and Paul whispers, "For now we see in a mirror, dimly."[11]

The coffee perks, she walks by your table, sunlight pours through the window. For a moment, some unknown hand draws back the veil behind which the best reality hides. For a moment, the hard fact, the bare-bones empirical, is peeled away to show the soft marrow of life. "A cleft has opened in the pitiless walls of the world," says C. S. Lewis, "and we are invited to follow our great Captain inside."[12]

Our hearts burn within us, and most of us spend our whole lives never knowing why. At the end of the day, I think it's because Christ is, always and everywhere, around us, singing. Once, shortly after Jesus had been crucified, some disciples of Jesus were traveling from village to village. Jesus came and walked with them, and they did not recognize him until that evening, when they ate dinner together and he blessed and broke the bread and their eyes were opened. And they then said to each other, "Did not our hearts burn within us while he talked to us on the road?"[13] Though they did not recognize Christ, their hearts burned within them. And I wonder if we would but ask, Christ would also open our eyes to see him?

○ ○ ○

It is a beautiful and difficult thing to work out your salvation. But don't just read more books about it. Start praying and start going to church. I know it sounds old-fashioned, but church is where Christian relationships bloom. Online sermons and books are all very well and good, but church is where Christian life takes shape. And if you haven't been to church in a while, don't start with a big suburban church. Their acres of parking lots and pews don't exactly imbue everyone-knows-your-name warm fuzzies. Find a cozy (and cell phone–free) walk-in-closet-sized church with so-bad-it's-good praise songs, and make yourself at home, sans the fancy pants.

Then get involved in their not-just-for-Sundays community life. And don't assume the worst. As every good Christian knows, life is brown. You don't have to sit at a white-linen-covered table and sip from crystal to enjoy good company. Just loosen your tie and pull up to the bar and down a couple of glugs, especially if it's something brown—something brandy or scotch or bourbon. No one will bat an eye. We Christians are, after all, broken and weary, but redeemed. We want to share the joy of holiness. We meet to worship and savor our Lord. We come to fit into Christ and each other and to make a life worth living. We come to drink and dance and sing, dammit.

People who can't stand hypocrisy often don't enjoy going to church. It is difficult to pretend to feel and to believe so many words and melodies you cannot touch or see except for a sample of wine and dry crackers. Besides, if there is a God, they might think, he does not need our guitars and creeds and deplorable prayers for forgiveness. I derive endless entertainment in concluding a pervasively

Christian book with the exhortation: Get thee to church! But a genuine life is better than a fake life. With the antique encouragement to go to church, it must also be said that, if you don't honestly thirst for God, don't go. But just because you might not earnestly want to go to church, don't assume everyone else is pretending. Church is not just a big show. God hasn't jumped up to heaven and accidentally locked himself inside. He came down to us and is working with what he has. He hasn't given up on humanity yet. And participation in his church is a doorway into becoming a part of his great artist's project.

Look out over your life. Listen to the people you love. Become attentive, and life will speak to you. God will speak to you. We often expect a sudden unveiling of absolute truth or safety. But it never comes, not in a trumpet blast or a sudden sky-lit flash. We have only the mumblings of our prayers and the bad sounds of our guitars and praise songs, our gestures at the altar. All we have is the summons to get involved in the muddy mess of Christian marriage, Christian friendships, Christian celibacy, and the overwhelming burden of daily life. But God has allowed (or, perhaps, orchestrated) it to be this way. And it is romantic and mundane; and it is holy and pitiful.

ACKNOWLEDGMENTS

This book is for Bryce. You are a good, good man.

This book is also for the Couch Society: Petrie, the Reverend Emrys, Ivan, Judson, Jared, Rob the Red Robin, Patrick, Michael the Poet, and you, Davey . . . or should I say, Ratty. As the Lord lives, go under the Mercy.

I would like to thank Evan Williams and Grain Belt for making affordable booze. And Emrys for smoking and covering my pages with red ink. And Sarah for taking the train to London just to explore and read my first draft. And Judson for visiting Minneapolis and looking things over. And also Spud (whom I love), Ivan, Viktorija, Rob, Gary, Steph, the Gaetano brothers, Laurel, Ron, my mom and dad, Katie, Tim and Heather, and my editors at Fresh Air Books. I love what Fresh Air Books is about. "Christian books for non-churchy people." That somehow describes me even though I go to church.

I am grateful for the very large G. K. Chesterton. And Josef Pieper, who is always at my bedside. C. S. Lewis is my teacher. I am also grateful for Charles Williams's study of Beatrice, Rollo May for his profound book *Love and Will*, Kenneth Grahame for *Wind in the Willows*, Eugene Peterson for *The Message*, Kahlil Gibran, A. G. Sertillanges (*The Intellectual Life* is my favorite book), John Dunne,

Robert Farrar Capon (who wrote the book I wish I wrote), Saint Bernard, Milton, Rainer Maria Rilke, and even Nygren, though his *Agape and Eros* synthesis is wrong. And E. E. Cummings, Gerard Manley Hopkins, Czeslaw Milosz, and the 1928 Book of Common Prayer. And Dante. I sit on the shoulders of giants, just taking it all in.

I would like to thank Dr. Michael Bauman, whose classroom not only challenges and questions but also encourages. My hand still aches from taking notes. My head aches too. I'd also like to thank Dr. Don Westblade and Hillsdale College's Christian Studies Department. And Dr. Smith, who lovingly gave me a D– on my first college essay, and introduced me to Dante. Dante and that D– changed my life. And the Rev., M.Div., B.A., B.S., and nearly B.C., Dr. John Reist. Thank you.

NOTES

Chapter 1: Mud & Poetry

1. I read this in Josef Pieper's essay "On Love" in *Faith, Hope, Love* (San Francisco: Ignatius Press, 1997), an insightful and informative essay on the subject. The study was conducted by René Spitz, author of "Hospitalism," in *The Psychoanalytic Study of the Child*, vol. 1 (London, 1945).

2. A similar case of psychosocial dwarfism can be found in Robert M. Sapolsky, *Why Zebras Don't Get Ulcers: A Guide to Stress, Stress-Related Diseases, and Coping* (New York: W. H. Freeman, 1994), 94–95. A dangerously underweight child was put under the care of a loving nurse. He gained weight and his growth hormone levels increased. Yet his emotional attachment to her was such that when she left, his hormone levels and weight would plummet, and when she returned, they would increase.

3. See Genesis 1:31.

4. The idea of mud and poetry is in some ways similar to the classical sentiment "dust and glory." Josef Pieper links Spitz's study to Erich Fromm's idea of "milk and honey" in *The Art of Loving* (New York, 1952). "Milk," to Fromm, is the symbol of the needs of life, while "honey" is the symbol of the sweetness and happiness of life. Milk and honey allude to the biblical metaphor of the promised land "flowing with milk and honey" (Exod. 3:8).

5. That is, this is not a new kind of dualism. It's a loose description of a spectrum.

6. Robert Friend, "My Cup," in *Dancing with a Tiger: Poems 1941–1998*, ed. Edward Field (London: Menard Press, 2003), 164.

7. See Romans 6:23.

8. In Matthew 10:28 Jesus contrasts the death of the body with death of both the body and soul: "Do not fear those who kill the body but cannot kill the soul; rather fear him who can destroy both soul and body in hell." The same idea appears in Luke 12:4-5. Ecclesiastes 12:7 speaks of mud and poetry: "The dust returns to the earth as it was, and the breath [or the spirit] returns to God who gave it." This refers back to Genesis 2:7, when God breathed the poetry of life into the mud from the ground, and Genesis 3:19: man shall return to mud.

9. Romans 8:21.

10. Genesis 3:22.

11. See Romans 7:14-25.

12. See Romans 5:12-21; 1 Corinthians 15:22; Psalms 51:5; 58:3.

13. See Romans 3:10-11; Ephesians 2:1-3.

14. See Psalm 139:7-8.

15. Saint Peter puts it beautifully: "By [God's] great mercy we have been born anew to a living hope through the resurrection of Jesus Christ from the dead, and to an inheritance which is imperishable, undefiled, and unfading, kept in heaven for you, who by God's power are guarded through faith for a salvation ready to be revealed in the last time" (1 Pet. 1:3-5, RSV).

16. See Romans 8:18, 29-30; 1 Peter 5:1, 4; 2 Corinthians 4:17.

17. See 1 Corinthians 15:54-56.

18. See 2 Corinthians 5:1-10; Philippians 1:19-26.

19. Ezekiel 18:4, 20, RSV.

20. George Herbert, "Mortification," in *The Complete English Poems*, ed. John Tobin (New York: Penguin, 2005), 91.

21. Lewis, *The Four Loves*, 2–3, italics mine.

22. Bernard of Clairvaux, *On Loving God*.

23. 1 John 4:19.

24. See John 17:1-5; Acts 2:33; 3:13-15; 5:31; Romans 6:4; Philippians 3:21; 1 Timothy 3:16; 1 Peter 1:21.

25. 1 John 3:2 (RSV). In Titus 2:13 (ESV) Saint Paul also speaks of "our blessed hope, the appearing of the glory of our great God and Savior Jesus Christ." Jesus prays in John 17:24 (RSV) that his disciples might even participate in his glory: "May [they] be with me where I am, to behold my glory which thou hast given me in thy love for me before the foundation of the world."

26. Romans 8:18; 2 Corinthians 4:17. The poet writes: "You guide me with your counsel, and afterward you will receive me to glory" (Ps. 73:24, ESV).

27. 1 Peter 5:4, ESV.

28. Bernard of Clairvaux, *On Loving God*.

29. "We ourselves, who have the firstfruits of the Spirit, groan inwardly as we wait eagerly for adoption as sons, the redemption of our bodies" (Rom. 8:23, ESV).

Chapter 2: Savvy-Bachelor Sex

1. Lewis, *The Four Loves*.
2. May, *Love and Will*, 57.
3. John Updike, "Wife-Wooing," *The Early Stories: 1953–1975* (New York: Ballantine, 2004), 350.
4. Harvey Cox, *The Secular City: Secularization and Urbanization in Theological Perspective* (New York: Collier Books, 1990), 175.
5. Ezekiel 37:9, paraphrased.
6. Neruda, "Body of a Woman," in *Twenty Love Poems*, 15.
7. Matthew 25:40, paraphrased.
8. Pieper, *Faith, Hope, Love*, 174.
9. Lewis, *The Weight of Glory*, 46.

Chapter 3: Saving My Pennies for a Motorcycle

1. Bonhoeffer, *Christ the Center*.
2. Bonaventure, *The Soul's Journey into God*, 108.
3. Czeslaw Milosz, *New and Collected Poems: 1931–2001* (New York: HarperCollins, 2001), 109.
4. See Proverbs 3:3; 6:21.
5. Colossians 3:16, NRSV; Proverbs 3:3, ESV.
6. Chesterton, *Orthodoxy*, 141.
7. While the "God-shaped vacuum" wording attributed to Pascal is widely accepted and copied, the actual wording of this thought from Pascal's *Pensées* is as follows: "What is it then that this desire and this inability proclaim to us, but that there was once in man a true happiness of which there now remain to him only the mark and empty trace, which he in vain tries to fill from all his surroundings, seeking from things absent the help he does not obtain in things present? But these are all inadequate, because the infinite abyss can only be filled by an infinite and immutable object, that is to say, only by God Himself" (Blase Pascal, *Pascal's Pensées* [Charleston, SC: BiblioLife, 2008], 115–16).
8. Revelation 19:6-7, NASB, italics mine.
9. Williams, *The Figure of Beatrice*, 38.
10. Romans 12:2, NIV.
11. 2 Corinthians 3:18, NIV.
12. Søren Kierkegaard, *Stages on Life's Way*, trans. Walter Lowrie (Princeton, NJ: Princeton University Press, 1967), 97.
13. See Ephesians 1:9-10.

Chapter 4: The Wienery

1. Mark Helprin, "Willis Avenue," in *A Dove of the East: And Other Stories* (New York: Knopf, 1975), 116.

2. Capon, *Bed and Board*, 71.

3. Wilfred Owen, "Dulce Et Decorum Est," in *The Collected Poems of Wilfred Owen* (New York: New Directions, 1965), 55.

4. George Meredith, "Hiding the Skeleton," in *Modern Love* (Whitefish, MT: Kessinger, 2005).

5. E. E. Cummings, *Poems 1923–1954*.

6. Vanauken, *A Severe Mercy*, 30.

7. John 1:46.

8. See Ephesians 1:9-10.

Chapter 5: Who's Got a Scar?

1. Isaiah 53:5, ESV.

2. See Romans 8:38-39.

3. John 4:16, NLT.

4. Luke 18:16.

5. Proverbs 5:22-23, NIV, italics mine.

6. Jeremiah 5:25, NIV, italics mine.

7. John 8:34, NIV.

8. 2 Corinthians 7:10, NIV.

9. Luke 23:40-41, paraphrased.

10. Luke 23:43.

11. Acts 3:19, NIV.

Chapter 6: Yoga Truth

1. 1 Timothy 1:15, NJB.

2. Huston Smith, introduction to *The Way of a Pilgrim*, trans. R. M. French (New York: Quality Paperback Club, 1998), ix.

3. Colossians 4:2, NIV.

4. Salinger, *Franny and Zooey*.

5. Psalm 105:4, NIV.

6. Matthew 5:48.

7. C. S. Lewis, *Mere Christianity* (New York: Collier Books/Macmillan, 1960), 169.

8. 1 Thessalonians 5:17.

9. 1 Thessalonians 5:18, NIV.

10. Matthew 6:7, NIV.

11. Luke 10:21, NJB.

12. Hesychios, *On Watchfulness and Holiness*, sec. 94, in Smith, *Philokalia*, 107.

13. See Matthew 3:2.

14. Romans 12:12, RSV.

15. Colossians 4:2, RSV.

16. Sertillanges, *The Intellectual Life*, 199.

17. Matthew 18:22, NIV.

Chapter 7: Crazy Love

1. Earle B. Fowler, *Spenser and the System of Courtly Love* (New York: Phaeton Press, 1968), 60–61.

2. Lewis, *The Allegory of Love*, 12.

3. Bernard of Clairvaux, *On Loving God*, 36.

4. Leclercq, *Monks on Marriage*, 2–4.

5. Dante Aligheri, *Purgatory*, vol. 2 of *The Divine Comedy*, trans. Charles Eliot Norton, canto 18 (Stilwell, KS: Digireads, 2005), 51.

6. Sir Osbert Sitwell's analogy, quoted in *Hell*, vol. 1 of Alighieri, *The Divine Comedy*, trans. Dorothy Sayers.

Chapter 8: A Galactic Pizza Person

1. See Matthew 28:19.

2. See Matthew 19:21.

3. Matthew 8:22, NASB.

4. Genesis 2:18, NIV.

5. Adrian Desmond and James Moore, *Darwin: The Life of a Tormented Evolutionist* (New York: W. W. Norton, 1994), 257–58.

6. See Genesis 2:23.

7. Robert Alter, quoted in Eldredge, *Wild at Heart*, 51.

8. Deuteronomy 33:26, NIV.

9. Søren Kierkegaard, *Stages on Life's Way*, trans. Howard V. Hong and Edna H. Hong (Princeton, NJ: Princeton University Press, 1988), 93.

10. Ephesians 5:25, 32, paraphrased.

11. Genesis 2:24.

12. 1 John 4:8.

13. Genesis 1:27.

14. Romans 12:5.

15. Williams, *The Figure of Beatrice*, 190.

16. See Matthew 25:40.

17. See Matthew 22:37-39.

18. Gibran, *The Prophet*, 7.

19. Ernest Thomson Seton and Julia M. Seton, comps., *The Gospel of the Redman: A Way of Life* (Santa Fe, NM: Seton Village, 1966), 18.

20. *Letters of Rainer Maria Rilke, 1910–1926*, trans. Jane Bannard Greene and M. D. Herter Norton (New York: W. W. Norton and Company, 1945), 65, 57.

21. Song of Solomon 6:3.

22. Genesis 28:16.

23. Genesis 28:17.

Chapter 9: How to Date Like a Christian

1. J. B. Priestley, *Talking: An Essay* (New York: Harper, 1926).
2. 1 Corinthians 7:9, NIV.
3. Matthew 25:14-30.
4. Gibran, *The Broken Wings,* 39.

Chapter 10: Brown Like Bourbon

1. John 10:10.
2. See Psalm 8:5; Hebrews 2:7.
3. Chesterton, *Orthodoxy,* 299.
4. Song of Solomon 8:1-2, paraphrased.
5. Song of Solomon 1:2.
6. Song of Solomon 1:3, NKJV.
7. Blaise Pascal, *The Works of Blaise Pascal* (Roslyn, NY: Black's Readers Service, 1941), 21.
8. Ecclesiastes 9:9, NASB.
9. Proverbs 5:18-19, NASB.
10. Song of Solomon 2:5, NKJV; see also Hosea 3:1.
11. Borrowed from Chesterton's metaphor for dogmatic doctrine in *Orthodoxy,* 215.
12. Kirk, Redeeming the Time.
13. I owe this metaphor to Mark Buchanan, *Your God Is Too Safe,* 54.
14. May, Love and Will, 96.
15. E. E. Cummings, *Poems 1923–1954.*

Chapter 11: When Kings Go Out to Battle

1. Gilder, *Men and Marriage,* 13.
2. Capon, *Bed and Board,* 62.
3. Genesis 1:28.
4. Genesis 4:12, KJV.
5. 2 Samuel 11:1, italics mine.
6. 2 Samuel 11:2.
7. 2 Samuel 11:4.
8. Henry Reed, "Naming of Parts," *New Statesman and Nations 24,* no. 598 (August 8, 1942): 92.
9. 2 Samuel 11:11.
10. 2 Samuel 12:1.
11. Gilder, *Men and Marriage,* 14.
12. Jean-Jacques Rousseau, *Emile, or On Education,* trans. Allan Bloom (New York: Basic Books, 1979), 358.
13. Steinbeck, *Travels with Charley,* 77.

14. See John 10:10.

15. Philippians 4:4, ESV.

16. Colossians 3:23, ESV.

Chapter 12: Jesus Is Sexual

1. Ephesians 5:25.

2. Ephesians 5:1.

3. Luke 2:49, KJV.

4. John 19:30.

5. John 17:21, paraphrased.

6. John 15:9.

7. Brennan Manning, *Ruthless Trust: The Ragamuffin's Path to God* (New York: HarperCollins, 2002), 69.

8. John 2:19, paraphrased.

9. John 8:7, paraphrased.

10. Ephesians 4:24, NLT.

11. John 17:18, *The Message*.

Chapter 13: Buddha and a Pragmatic Catamaran

1. Chesterton, *The Everlasting Man*, 62.

2. The seven sacraments: the rites of baptism, confirmation, the Eucharist, penance, anointing of the sick, ordination, and matrimony.

3. Bonaventure, *The Soul's Journey into God*, 26.

4. Hebrews 11:1.

5. Romans 1:20, NASB.

6. Fyodor Dostoyevsky, *The Brothers Karamazov*, trans. Richard Pevear and Larissa Volokhonsky (New York: Farrar, Straus, 1990), 108.

7. Williams, *The Figure of Beatrice*, 10; Lewis, *Transposition*, 138.

8. Gerard Manley Hopkins, "God's Grandeur," in *Poems and Prose*, 27.

9. Ibid.

10. Isaiah 6:3, NIV.

11. 1 Corinthians 13:12.

12. Lewis, *The Weight of Glory*, 45.

13. Luke 24:32, ESV.

BIBLIOGRAPHY

Alighieri, Dante. *The Divine Comedy*. Translated by Mark Musa. New York: Penguin, 1995.

———. *The Divine Comedy*. Translated by Dorothy Sayers. New York: Penguin, 1949.

Aristotle. *The Politics*. Translated by Carnes Lord. Chicago: University of Chicago Press, 1984.

Augustine. *The Confessions*. Translated by F. J. Sheed. Cambridge: Hackett, 1943.

Barber, Richard. *The Knight and Chivalry*. London: Cardinal Press, 1974.

Berry, Wendell. *The Unsettling of America*. San Francisco: Sierra Club, 1977.

Bernard of Clairvaux. *On Loving God*. Edited by Hugh Martin. London: SCM Press, 1959.

Bonaventure. *The Soul's Journey Into God*. Translated by Ewert H. Cousins. Mahwah, NJ: Paulist Press, 1978.

Bonhoeffer, Dietrich. *Christ the Center*. New York: HarperSanFrancisco, 1978.

———. *Life Together*. New York: Harper and Row, 1954.

Brianchaninov, Ignatius. *On the Prayer of Jesus.* Boston: New Seed Books, 2006.

Brown, Harold O. J. *Heresies.* Grand Rapids: Hendrickson, 2003.

Buchanan, Mark. *Your God Is Too Safe: Rediscovering the Wonder of a God You Can't Control.* Sisters, OR: Multnomah, 2001.

Capellanus, Andreas. *The Art of Courtly Love.* New York: Columbia University Press, 1960.

Capon, Robert Farrar. *Bed and Board: Plain Talk About Marriage.* New York: Simon and Shuster, 1965.

Cherchi, Paolo. *Andreas and the Ambiguity of Courtly Love.* London: University of Toronto Press, 1994.

Chesterton, G. K. *The Everlasting Man.* Radford, VA: Wilder Publications, 2008.

———. *Heretics.* London: Butler and Tanner, 1928.

———. *Orthodoxy.* London: Hodder and Stoughton, 1999.

———. *St. Thomas Aquinas.* New York: Image Books, 1956.

Cox, Harvey. *The Feast of Fools.* Cambridge: Harvard University Press, 1969.

———. *The Secular City: Secularization and Urbanization in Theological Perspective.* New York: Collier Books, 1990.

Cummings, E. E. *Poems 1923–1954.* New York: Harcourt, Brace, 1954.

Donne, John. *The Major Works.* Edited by John Carey. New York: Oxford University Press, 1990.

Dostoyevsky, Fyodor. *The Brothers Karamazov.* Translated by Richard Pevear and Larissa Volokhonsky. New York: Farrar, Straus, 1990.

Eldredge, John. *Wild at Heart: Discovering the Secret of a Man's Soul.* Nashville: Thomas Nelson, 2001.

Eldredge, John, and Brent Curtis. *The Sacred Romance.* Nashville: Thomas Nelson, 1997.

Erickson, Millard J. *Christian Theology.* Grand Rapids: Baker Books, 1996.

Eliot, T. S. *Complete Poems and Plays 1909–1950*. New York: Harcourt Brace, 1967.

Evans, Dylan. *Emotion: A Very Short Introduction*. New York: Oxford University Press, 2001.

Francis de Sales. *Introduction to the Devout Life*. Translated by John K. Ryan. New York: Harper and Row, 1966.

French, R. M., trans. *The Way of the Pilgrim*. New York: Quality Paper Back Book Club, 1998.

Grahame, Kenneth. *The Wind in the Willows*. New York: Scribner, 1961.

Gibran, Kahlil. *The Prophet*. Hertfordshire: Wordsworth, 1996.

Gibran, Kahlil. *The Broken Wings*. New York: The Citadel Press, 1957.

Gilder, George. *Men and Marriage*. Gretna, LA: Pelican, 1992.

Gregory of Nyssa. *The Life of Moses*. Translated by Abraham J. Malherbe and Everett Ferguson. New York: Paulist Press, 1978.

Heschel, Abraham Joshua. *The Sabbath*. New York: Farrar, Straus, 2005.

Hopkins, Gerard Manley. *Poems and Prose*. New York: Penguin, 1963.

Kass, Amy A., and Leon R. Kass. *Wing to Wing, Oar to Oar*. Notre Dame: University of Notre Dame, 2000.

Keen, Maurice. *Chivalry*. New Haven: Yale University Press, 1984.

Kierkegaard, Søren. *Works of Love*. New York: Harper and Row, 1962.

Kirk, Russell. *Redeeming the Time*. Edited by Jeffrey O. Nelson. Wilmington, DE: Intercollegiate Studies Institute, 1996.

Leclercq, Jean. *Monks on Marriage: A Twelfth-Century View*. New York: Seabury Press, 1982.

Lewis, C. S. *The Allegory of Love: A Study in Medieval Tradition*. New York: Oxford University Press, 1958.

———. *The Four Loves*. New York: Harcourt, 1988.

————. *A Preface to Paradise Lost.* New York: Oxford University Press, 1961.

————. *The Screwtape Letters.* London: Fount Press, 1979.

————. *Transposition and Other Addresses.* London: Geoffrey Bles, 1949.

————. *The Weight of Glory.* New York: HarperSanFrancisco, 1949.

Lossky, Vladimir. *Orthodox Theology.* New York: St. Vladimir's Seminary Press, 1978.

May, Rollo. *Love and Will.* New York: W.W. Norton, 1969.

Milton, John. *Paradise Lost.* Edited by Alastair Fowler. London: Longman, 1998.

"Monk of the Eastern Church," *The Jesus Prayer.* New York: St. Vladimir's Seminary Press, 1987.

Mood, John J. L. *Rainer Maria Rilke On Love and Other Difficulties.* New York: W.W. Norton, 1975.

Mott, Lewis Freeman. *The System of Courtly Love.* New York: Haskell House, 1965.

Neruda, Pablo. *Twenty Love Poems and a Song of Despair.* Translated by W. S. Merwin. San Francisco: Chronicle Books, 1993.

Neuhaus, Richard John. *The Eternal Pity.* Notre Dame: University of Notre Dame Press, 2000.

Newman, John Henry. *The Idea of a University.* Notre Dame: University of Notre Dame Press, 2003.

Noble, Peter. *Love and Marriage in Chrétien de Troyes.* Cardiff: University of Wales Press, 1982.

Nygren, Anders. *Agape and Eros.* Translated by A. G. Hebert. New York: Macmillan, 1941.

Peterson, Eugene. *The Message.* Colorado Springs: NavPress, 2006.

Pieper, Josef. *Faith, Hope, Love.* San Francisco: Ignatius Press, 1997.

————. *In Tune with the World.* South Bend, IN: St. Augustine's Press, 1999.

————. *Leisure: The Basis of Culture.* South Bend, IN: St. Augustine's Press, 1998.

Pseudo-Dionysius. Translated by Colm Luibheid. New York: Paulist Press, 1987.

Quell, Gottfried, and Ethelbert Stauffer. *LOVE*. London: Adam and Charles Black, 1933.

Rahner, Hugo. *Man at Play*. New York: Herder and Herder, 1967.

Rilke, Rainer Maria. *Letters to a Young Poet*. Translated by M. D. Herter Norton. New York: W.W. Norton, 1962.

Salinger, J. D. *Franny and Zooey*. New York: Bantam, 1962.

Schaeffer, Francis A. *Genesis in Space and Time*. Downers Grove: InterVarsity Press, 1972.

Sertillanges, A. G. *The Intellectual Life: Its Spirit, Conditions, Methods*. Translated by Mary Ryan. Westminster, MD: Newman Press, 1946.

Smith, Allyne. *Philokalia: The Eastern Christian Spiritual Texts*. Woodstock, NY: SkyLight, 2006.

Steinbeck, John. *Travels with Charley and Later Novels, 1947–1962*. New York: Library of America, 2007.

Tillich, Paul. *Love, Power, and Justice*. New York: Oxford University Press, 1954.

Vanauken, Sheldon. *A Severe Mercy*. San Francisco: HarperSanFrancisco, 1987.

Wangerin, Walter, Jr. *The Book of God*. Grand Rapids: Zondervan, 1996.

Ware, Kallistos. *The Orthodox Way*. New York: St. Vladimir's Seminary Press, 1979.

Williams, Charles. *The Figure of Beatrice*. Berkeley, CA: Apocryphile Press, 2005.

———. *He Came Down from Heaven and The Forgiveness of Sins*. Berkeley, CA: Apocryphile Press, 2005.

———. *Outlines of Romantic Theology*. Berkeley, CA: Apocryphile Press, 2005.

———. *Religion and Love in Dante*. Westminster: Dacre Press, 1941.

ABOUT THE AUTHOR

TYLER BLANSKI grew up in Minneapolis, Minnesota. He graduated from the Perpich Center for Arts Education (2002); studied at the Center for Medieval and Renaissance Studies, Oxford, England (2005); and holds a bachelor of arts in Christian Studies from Hillsdale College (2006). He is a cofounder of Venite Ministries, a Christian spiritual formation resource and retreat center in Minneapolis, and cofounder of the Couch Society, a theological forum and journal.

In addition to *Mud and Poetry*, Tyler has written three other books (including a book of poetry) and released two albums: *Think Out Loud: Music Fighting Homelessness* and *Out from the Darkness*. He lives in Uptown Minneapolis, where he manages a small house-painting business, Rembrandt Home Painting; participates in the communal life of an Anglican church; and writes. For more information, visit Tyler's Web sites: www.mudandpoetry.com or www.tyler blanski.com.